THINGS THAT PERTAIN TO THE SPIRIT

by
Dr. Ed Dufresne

rockhousepublishing
sellersburg • indiana

Unless otherwise indicated, all Scripture quotations are taken from the *King James Version* of the Bible.

Scripture quotations marked AMP are taken from the *Amplified® Bible*, Copyright © 1954, 1958, 1962, 1964, 1965, 1987 by The Lockman Foundation. Used by permission.

Cover Design by: Wilson Design & Publishing

Things That Pertain to the Spirit
ISBN: 978-0-94076-326-5
Copyright © 2008 by Ed Dufresne Ministries
P.O. Box 1010
Murrieta, CA 92564
U.S.A.

1st Printing
2500/2500

Published by Ed Dufresne Ministries
P.O. Box 1010
Murrieta, CA 92564
U.S.A.

DEDICATION

I dedicate this book to the Body of Christ. You are the ones God has chosen. You are the ones in whom God has invested His all-conquering power. I challenge you to take these mighty gifts of the Spirit, become skillful with them, and go forward doing exploits!

TABLE OF CONTENTS

INTRODUCTION

1 Corinthians 12:1
Now concerning spiritual *gifts*, brethren,
I would not have you ignorant.

When you read this scripture, it's important to understand the fullness of what's being said. The original Greek actually reads, "Now concerning things that pertain to the Spirit." The word "gifts" is italicized, which means it was added by the King James interpreters. They did that to help us understand the meaning of the verse, but I don't think they helped us in this case. God doesn't want us to be ignorant of *all* things that pertain to the Spirit, not just the gifts of the Spirit. This entire chapter in First Corinthians is talking about living in the Spirit and understanding spiritual things. It begins with the gifts of the Spirit, and then talks about the body of Christ and offices of ministry. These are all spiritual things we don't want to be ignorant about.

We also see this verse starts with the word "now." It doesn't say, "Now back in that day." It says "now" because it relates to today. The Bible is relevant, and what it says hasn't passed away (Matthew 24:35). We can call on these things that pertain to the Spirit because they are available to us today.

1 Corinthians 12:1, AMP.
Now about the spiritual gifts (the special endowments of supernatural energy), brethren, I do not want you to be MISINFORMED.

Some people think these things have passed away because they're either uninformed or misinformed. A person who is "uninformed" is a person who has never been taught and doesn't know these things exist. A person who is "misinformed" has been taught wrong about these things. Being ignorant or misinformed about things that pertain to the Spirit can hurt you.

"WHEN I WAS IN *Heaven*..."

In October of 1999 I went to Heaven. I had just finished a service in Oakland, California, and was getting ready to take the elevator to the fellowship hall in the church building. When the doors to the elevator closed, it felt like I was being pulled out of my body. The last thing I remember was saying, "I don't know if I can go that far."

Suddenly, I was in Heaven, face down before the throne of God. One of the things God talked to me about while there was Hebrews 2:4.

Hebrews 2:4
God also bearing *them* witness, both with signs and wonders, and with divers miracles, and gifts of the Holy Ghost, according to his own will?

Hebrews 2:4, AMP.
[Besides this evidence] it was also

8

established and plainly endorsed by God, Who showed His approval of it by signs and wonders and various miraculous manifestations of [His] power and by imparting the gifts of the Holy Spirit [to the believers] according to His own will.

God said He was about ready to distribute – distribute endowments. That was when Jesus laid His hands on my head and I received an endowment to kill cancer. He said that endowment would begin at a certain percentage of success and then increase. He also told me there will be a time when that endowment will operate at full potential power in my meetings. Glory to God, I am starting to see it more and more! We have had a high percentage of people healed of cancer. Even those given only days to live! But this isn't just for me and my ministry. God said there would be others who will go around the earth with special endowments from Heaven. This is for those ministries and churches where people believe. God wants to distribute these endowments, but we can't be ignorant of how they operate (Matthew 22:29).

In 1999, the same year I went to Heaven, that wave of glory and endowments began to go out. It's also the time the devil came in with the modernistic church to try and distract us from the true move of God. That's why the devil started getting Christians stirred up in 2006 to speak against ministers and their money. Satan wants us to be so busy dealing with these distractions that we miss out on the things pertaining to the Spirit of God. These attacks can be a distraction if we don't understand how the devil operates. The devil can't hinder us from carrying out God's plan in the earth, only we can.

The devil is like a skunk you hit out on a country road. The skunk may be dead, but his stink is still around. I am not saying the devil is dead. He uses that stink to make you think he's still around, but he has to go when you say go!

We have to guard against being distracted and aborting what God wants to do. The Welsh revival of 1904 was aborted. It was a powerful move of God in Wales. But the leader, Evan Roberts, began listening to a "prophetess" who got him off pursuing the wrong things and quenched that revival. I believe that revival came over to California where they had the Azusa Street revival.

You see, God will come to hungry people. It doesn't matter if they are denominational folks, Pentecostal folks, whoever! God doesn't want a church with a bunch of big religious fat heads. He wants people hungry for the things of God. He wants people like Smith Wigglesworth who moved the world from his small home in Manchester, England. He went all over the world, and people still talk about his ministry today because it was done in the Spirit. He was a man of the Spirit. I don't want to play church, do you? If we want to *be* the church, instead of *playing* church, we have to be people of the Spirit!

THE *Azusa* STREET REVIVAL (1906-1915)

I was recently reading a book from a man who interviewed those who were children in the Azusa Street revival. They said that William Seymour, a leader in the revival, would come out with a box over his head. A box! People in today's churches wouldn't stand for that. They would be complaining about "that preacher with a box over his head". They would never meet in an old livery stable and sit on planks and crates for pews. Believe me, there was nothing nice about that revival, but it shook the world! That revival birthed the Assembly of God and Church of God churches. That revival had a lasting effect because it was of the Spirit.

The man who wrote that book actually showed up at my meeting in Pawnee, Oklahoma. He said that as he interviewed these people for his book, they spoke about Brother Seymour having that box on his head. They said when he did that, the glory of God came in so thick the children would play hide-and-seek in it. You see, I was taught that the Azusa Street revival was only a move of the baptism in the Holy Ghost, but God gave people who were missing limbs new body parts in that glory. God has His way of doing things. Some people would call a preacher with a box on his head foolish; but if God wants to perform a creative miracle in that environment, who are we to say it's wrong?

> THAT REVIVAL HAD A LASTING EFFECT BECAUSE IT WAS OF THE *Spirit*.

1 Corinthians 1:27
But God hath chosen the foolish things of the world to confound the wise; and God hath chosen the weak things of the world to confound the things which are mighty;

I've been seeing the glory in my meetings, but not in the depth they did in 1906. I tell you what though, God is going to do it again! In 1910 both William Seymour and Charles Parham, at a separate revival, prophesied some things that confirmed what I saw while in Heaven. They both said in 100 years there would be a revival of a greater measure than Azusa Street. We are hip deep in that glory now, but by 2010 it will be over our heads. We will be in the full potential of the anointing! When the wave of God's power comes in, the water goes up!

"...A *New Era* HAS BEGUN"

When attending the memorial service for my spiritual father, Kenneth E. Hagin, the Spirit of the Lord said to me, "An era has come to an end, and a new era has begun." God said some of us will have to continue what Dad Hagin was leading us into – getting people into the things of the Spirit. Many are going a different direction. Many are going a way he told us not to go. We have to be *Word* and *Spirit* churches, not churches that compromise the message! We must hunger for the things of the Spirit, not just hunger for numbers. We don't covet these things for ourselves so we can be big shots. We hunger for them to help others and to profit withal (1 Corinthians 12:7). Things happen in the lives of hungry people: in their businesses, their families, and their finances.

> AN ERA HAS COME TO AN END AND A *New* ERA HAS BEGUN.

The future holds miracles. The future holds the glory. The future holds the precious fruit of the earth (James 5:7). This will be an era of the gifts of the Spirit like the earth has never seen, but we need to walk with God. We need to worship God and look to Him as our supply financially, and look to Him to supply our buildings. It's all available to us in these last days. When we walk with God and believe, we will be a magnet for good things. But we can't be ignorant of how God does things, and we have to hunger for them!

A MAN WHO *Spit*

There was one man at the turn of the century with an endowment for creative miracles. He was not a very educated man, but his wife helped him learn to read. One day he got to the place in the Bible where Jesus spit on a deaf and dumb man, and he was healed.

> **Mark 7:32-35**
> **And they bring unto him one that was deaf, and had an impediment in his speech; and they beseech him to put his hand upon him. And he took him aside from the multitude, and put his fingers into his ears, and HE SPIT, and touched his tongue; And looking up to heaven, he sighed, and saith unto him, Ephphatha, that is, Be opened. And straightway his ears were opened, and the string of his tongue was loosed, and he spake plain.**

This man started praying for people and spitting on them. He would rub spit on a person with no arm and a new arm would grow out. These things worked for this man because he believed. He was hungry for them!

A man once told me he would never let a person spit on him. I said, "If I didn't have an arm, he could spit on me all he wanted because I could always wash it off." The man who said that is a fool! He's not the kind of person who will receive these things. We will see more creative miracles for those willing to believe and not bound by religion (Mark 7:13). Never criticize the way God's power is manifested or how God uses a person.

WHAT'S THE *Hold Up*?

We've been talking about having revival for years. I have to ask, "What's the hold up?" Sadly, the answer is *us*! We're in some things spiritually, but we are coming more fully into them. Do you feel it? I do.

God is now allowing me to talk about some of these things. I feel I have a responsibility to teach these things because there aren't many who teach on it. That's why so many ministers are coming to us and wanting our teaching. I want to help ministers finish their course. My wife and I want to teach people to have longevity and joy in life. And we're doing it!

As you read this book, you'll receive revelation and impartations by the power of God. When you're in a prophet's room, revelation comes to you (1 Kings 19:16). The Holy Ghost brings revelation, but this is different. Just because I'm not prophesying doesn't mean I'm not flowing in the prophet's ministry. When I speak from the prophet's office, those words go deeper into your spirit. As people understand the things of the Spirit, it will help them know the gifts of the Spirit, their supply, and their part in the body of Christ. It profits them. I believe you're one of those people.

_____

I WANT TO HELP MINISTERS *Fin-ish* THEIR COURSE.

_____

Say this out loud before reading this book...

"With the help of the Holy Ghost, I'm going to operate in these spiritual laws. I don't want to be ignorant. I'm getting more knowledge for this revival and how to flow in it."

CHAPTER One

"I WOULD NOT HAVE YOU IGNORANT"

1 Corinthians 12:1
Now concerning spiritual *gifts*, brethren,
I would not have you ignorant.

I don't know about things pertaining to the Spirit just because I'm a prophet; I know about these things because I'm a believer. I've noticed through forty-three years of ministry that most Christians live in their minds and their flesh. Some Christians seem to be moved by everything *but* the Spirit of God. Living like that will cause you not to profit from the things of the Spirit (Romans 8:6).

Let's look at First Corinthians 12:1 from the Amplified Bible.

"Now about the spiritual gifts (the special endowments of supernatural energy), brethren, I do not want you to be MISINFORMED."

If I was ignorant of electricity, I wouldn't mess with it. I remember one time when I was younger; I got under my house to fix something electrical. It was damp, and I got myself electrocuted. I thought I was dead! That was ignorance.

How about taking a motor apart and putting it back together when you have no mechanical understanding? What about the power of movement? If you're ignorant of the power of a moving car and you get in front of it, it will cause damage. The same thing holds true for the power of God. When you're ignorant, there are consequences.

> **Hosea 4:6**
> **My people are destroyed for lack of knowledge...**

We're destroyed by our ignorance of spiritual things. We have come so far in the natural realm and the educating of our minds, but know so little about the things of the Spirit. Think of it, years ago Benjamin Franklin saw lightning and wondered if he could harness it. Then a man named Thomas Edison used that knowledge to create the light bulb. Today we can put a man on the moon, but there's still so much ignorance about the things of God.

How about people who can't tell the difference between a person operating by the Spirit of God and a person operating with a familiar spirit? It's not a matter of the discerning of spirits; it's simple discernment that every Christian should have! You have some of these guys on television operating by a familiar spirit one night and the Spirit of God the next, and the believers watching don't even know it! Sometimes the minister doesn't even know it!

WHEN YOU'RE *Ignorant*, THERE ARE CONSEQUENCES.

I had a new believer in our Las Vegas church tell me he was watching a woman ministering on television and something on the inside said, "What she's saying isn't right." He told me her name and I told him, "You heard right." That man was only seven months old in the Lord, yet there are Christians who have been saved thirty-five years who fall for that stuff. Always remember, anyone who comes along just to get money out of you is wrong. People have to be taught right!

Every Christian's questions can be answered by the Bible. When there's a problem, it's because a believer is ignorant or doesn't want to do what the Bible says. People are destroyed in their finances because they don't know what the Bible says. They may claim to have knowledge, but then they won't tithe. They say, "I tried it and it didn't work." You don't try spiritual things, you do them!

BE A *Doer* OF THE WORD OF GOD

Whatever the Word says, I'm going to do it. When you go to a good church and receive right teaching but refuse to do it, you're in rebellion to God. You're responsible to do the Word when you hear it. It's ignorance for a person to see something in the Word, hear it preached, and *not* do it. There are no excuses in Heaven for not knowing when you have been taught.

If you don't violate what the Word says, it will work. God will answer your prayers, but you have to read the instructions (1 John 5:14-15).

Have you ever noticed how some men like to put their kid's bike together without looking at the instructions? They say, "Looking at the directions is a waste of time. I can do it myself." People in the church do the same thing. They think they can figure God out with their carnal minds instead of getting in their Bibles and seeing what God says about things.

You may be thinking, what does this have to do with things that pertain to the Spirit? Well, the Word of God is spirit *and* life, and we're told to walk in the Spirit (Galatians 5:16). Walking in the Spirit means walking according to the Word of God. We have to walk in the Spirit every day. To do that, you'll have to renew your mind according to the Word of God.

> **Romans 12:1 & 2**
> **I beseech you therefore, brethren, by the mercies of God, that ye present your bodies a living sacrifice, holy, acceptable unto God, *which is* your reasonable service. And be not conformed to this world: but BE YE TRANSFORMED BY THE RENEWING OF YOUR MIND, that ye may prove what *is* that good, and acceptable, and perfect, will of God.**

Refusing to renew your mind is ignorant. Remember back during the Charismatic revival? Some people thought you had to tarry for the baptism in the Holy Ghost. Thank God, today we know better! Right after I got saved, I was being prayed for to receive the Holy Ghost, and there were three people talking to me. One was saying, "Let go." Another said, "Hold on." The third person told me, "Say Coca-Cola over and over." Talk about confusing! Praise God we're not there anymore, but we still have some things to learn.

We're the most educated generation since Pentecost, but still the most ignorant in some things pertaining to the Spirit. We have to mortify the deeds of the flesh and renew our minds by praying in the Holy Ghost and getting in our Bibles. It's up to you. I report; you decide!

God told me that ninety percent of His children live beneath what He provided for them. That way of living happens when people don't live in the Spirit and don't do what the Word says. I don't know about you, but I'm going to be in that ten percent that receives. I'm also going to help make that percentage higher by preaching the Word of God.

OPERATOR, *Administrator*, MANIFESTOR

Every gift, every operation, and every manifestation of the Spirit has a job description. Do you know what they are? Sometimes, Spirit-filled believers want to shake all these things together and mix them up, but there are differences. Look at First Corinthians 12:7. *"But the manifestation of the Spirit is given to every man TO PROFIT WITHAL."*

Lumping all these things together hurts our understanding of how they work. We can't "profit withal" without being properly taught in these areas. What does the Word have to say? Let's look at First Corinthians 12:4-7 and educate ourselves.

> **1 Corinthians 12:4**
> **Now there are diversities of gifts, but the same Spirit.**

The gifts of the Spirit vary, but the Holy Ghost stays the

same. Some people are teaching there are three Holy Spirits, but there is only One.

> **1 Corinthians 12:5**
> **And there are differences of ADMINISTRATIONS, but the same Lord.**

Jesus is in charge of administration. We would call him the *administrator* of these endowments and gifts. He's the Head of the church and the One who distributes spiritual gifts to those in the body of Christ (Ephesians 5:23). Jesus distributes all spiritual endowments, not just the gifts of the Spirit.

> **1 Corinthians 12:6**
> **And there are diversities of OPERATIONS, but it is the same God which worketh all in all.**

God is the operator of the universe. He has the "master plan" for what He would like done.

> **1 Corinthians 12:7**
> **But the MANIFESTATION of the Spirit is given to every man to profit withal.**

The Holy Spirit's job is to help manifest these giftings and endowments. God is the operator, Jesus is the administrator, and the Holy Ghost is the manifestor. What God wants done, Jesus administrates to those in the church, and the Holy Ghost manifests it. For the Holy Ghost to manifest, however, He has to do it through the body of Christ. The Holy Spirit is our Helper, not our doer. He can't do it without us because Satan still has the earth's lease from

I WOULD NOT HAVE YOU IGNORANT

Adam (Genesis 3:15). That's why we have to be yielded to the Spirit. That's why praying in the Holy Ghost is so important. God can have it planned out, Jesus can endow us to do it, the Holy Ghost can be waiting to manifest it; but if we're not yielded, we can hinder the whole process. Are you hindering or helping God's plan in your life? Are you producing any fruit?

Fruit PRODUCERS

When we're yielded to the Spirit of God and His plan, there will be fruit in our lives. I asked my people at our Saturday Night Live service, "What are you taking to Heaven with you?" People can say what they want, but the only thing they're taking to Heaven is their fruit! God is interested in us leaving the earth with fruit. It's not just about having numbers or being known; God wants fruit!

A few years back I had a minister friend tell some people that Jesus was coming back in 2007. They asked what I thought, and I took them to Mark 13:7. *"And when ye shall hear of wars and rumours of wars, be ye not troubled: for such things must needs be; but the end shall not be yet."*

I know there's a lot going on in the earth today, but the time is not yet. The precious fruit of the earth isn't in.

> **James 5:7**
> **Be patient therefore, brethren, unto the coming of the Lord. Behold, the husbandman waiteth for the precious fruit of the earth, and hath long patience for it, until he receive the early and latter rain.**

The Holy Spirit isn't going to leave the earth and go to Heaven without fruit! He isn't going to come before God empty-handed! He's going to bring the precious fruit of the earth back to Heaven when He returns!

I don't want to seem disrespectful, but if what we've seen in the last few years is all there is to this end-time revival, I'm heading straight to the head office when I get to Heaven. I want to know, "Is this it? Was that it? That was the big pop? What about the prophecy of Smith Wigglesworth weeping over Lester Sumrall where he saw the hospitals emptying out and the glory moving in? What about everything Dad Seymour said about another revival in 2010?" God told me I'd be a part of that end-time revival, and this is not it! There is fruit to be had!

Our fruit is important to God. Sometimes it means more to God than we think. I remember Dad Hagin pleading with God about his wife when she was facing a serious physical condition. While praying, he reminded God of his merits, his fruit.

> **Isaiah 43:26, AMP.**
> **Put Me in remembrance [REMIND ME OF YOUR MERITS]; let us plead *and* argue together. Set forth your case, that you may be justified (proved right).**

Dad Hagin reminded God of his merits, that he had left his home and family to serve in ministry. He reminded God of the times he obeyed and did what God told him to do. He brought his fruit to God, and God answered his prayer.

Do you have any fruit? Do you have any merits? Do you have any works to bring to God? People who do what

I WOULD NOT HAVE YOU IGNORANT

the Word of God says sure do!

CHAPTER Two

"FOR THIS CAUSE"

1 Corinthians 12:1
Now concerning spiritual *gifts*, brethren,
I would not have you ignorant.

First Corinthians was a letter written by the apostle Paul. He didn't include the chapters and verses when writing; they were added later to help us find certain scriptures. Sometimes the chapters and verses don't help too much because we stop reading at the end of a chapter and miss what God is trying to say in the next chapter. To get a better idea of what Paul was telling us in First Corinthians 12:1, let's back up a few verses and begin reading.

1 Corinthians 11:29-31, 12:1
For he that eateth and drinketh
unworthily, eateth and drinketh
damnation to himself, not discerning the
Lord's body. FOR THIS CAUSE many
***are* weak and sickly among you, and**
many sleep. For if we would judge
ourselves, we should not be judged. Now
concerning spiritual *gifts*, brethren, I
would not have you ignorant.

Paul said, "For this *cause...*" Have you ever noticed some people never know why things happen? They ask, "Why did God do that?" or "How did that happen?" Spirit-filled believers should never be left in the dark about things in their lives! There's always a cause for the things that take place, and those causes are spiritual in nature. God doesn't want us to be ignorant of spiritual things, and that includes causes that open the door to the devil.

In First Corinthians 11:29-12:1 Paul said, "For *this* cause..." There is a specific cause for many being weak, sickly, and many dying prematurely. What is the cause? Not discerning the Lord's body. That can mean not discerning what Jesus did in *His* body on the cross. It can mean not discerning *your* part in the body of Christ. Or it can mean not discerning the part that *others* have in the body of Christ.

Look again at what Paul wrote. "Many are weak and sickly *among you*, and many sleep." This is the church he's talking to! The group that should be the most educated about spiritual things and understanding the Lord's body! Is that you? Do you get weak physically or financially? Do you get sick? If so, you had better deal with it before you get to the next step, which is premature death! If I have those problems, I find out the cause. I ask myself, "Am I walking in love?" If I'm not walking in love, the devil has a right to come in. If I'm disobedient to the Word or God's house, Satan has a way to come in. But if we judge ourselves by the Word of God, we will not be judged.

> SPIRIT-FILLED BELIEVERS SHOULD NEVER BE LEFT IN THE *Dark* ABOUT THINGS IN THEIR LIVES!

1 Corinthians 11:31
For if we would judge ourselves, we
should not be judged.

I know of men who split churches, and in five to ten years they were dead, messed up or divorced. Those men broke a spiritual law when they split those churches. They hurt their pastors. They hurt the body of Christ. If a Christian dies premature or is not making it, there's always a cause.

SOME *Causes*

TITHING

Tithing is a spiritual thing (Malachi 3:7-14).

Hebrews 7:8
And here men that die receive tithes; but
there he *receiveth them*, of whom it is
witnessed that he liveth.

When you don't bring your tithe, you're not discerning the Lord's body. Years ago, I learned I needed to tithe. I didn't have a problem doing it. When I got saved, it felt like God took two semi-trucks off my back. I figured the least I could do is honor Him with my tithe. You don't have to fall off the lettuce truck too many times to figure that out!

I know I've been blessed by the operation of tithing and giving offerings. I'm blessed because I properly discerned the Lord's body in that area. My wife and I have a beautiful home and nice cars. God told me to build a twelve car garage and that He would fill it up. He also said to build two apartment suites above the garage, and take care of ministers. I obeyed, and He blessed me because of it. I don't need anything for me. God supplies all my need. But I still have to be right in these areas. But not everybody is.

Have you ever noticed how some people get blessed financially, then suddenly find a fault in their church and leave? They didn't really find a fault; they just wanted to get out of giving their part financially. One way to tell if a person is right in this area is by what they do when they sell their home and make a profit. Do they tithe, or are they stingy? Stingy people hurt what God wants to do in the earth when they don't tithe. You're flesh-minded when you don't want to hear about tithing and hear about discerning your part in the local church. Those are the kinds of people who start tithing but quit when the devil puts a little pressure on their finances. That's why there's weakness, sickness, and death in their finances. Quitters are a dime a dozen! I'm not a quitter! Are you?

UNFORGIVENESS

Many are weak, sick, and die prematurely due to unforgiveness. Unforgiveness is a spiritual cause of how the devil can get in.

> **2 Corinthians 2:10 & 11**
> **To whom ye forgive any thing, I *forgive* also: for if I forgave any thing, to whom I forgave *it*, for your sakes *forgave I it* in the person of Christ; Lest Satan should get an advantage of us: for we are not ignorant of his devices.**

Satan can take advantage of a person when they don't

forgive. Matthew 18:34 says people who don't forgive are delivered over to the "tormentors". Someone else may not repent for what they did, but you still have to forgive them for it! You hurt yourself when you're in unforgiveness. If the Word teaches it, you're responsible for it. The Word teaches walking in

IF THE *Word* TEACHES IT, YOU'RE RESPONSIBLE OR IT.

love, and you're responsible for it. God won't *make* you forgive anybody; you have to *choose* to forgive.

It's amazing how people always have to let somebody know how they got hurt. That's nothing more than unforgiveness. They just want to get you contaminated with it too! Don't do it! Don't be ignorant of what the devil is trying to do through that person. You may love that person and they may be a Christian, but don't get caught up in their unforgiveness. It will always cost you more than you want to pay.

I know it will cost you because I've been out of God's will in this area. There was one time when I just knew everything wasn't popping. It was like I had eight cylinders, but only four were working! I asked God about it, and He said it was because I got mad at a person in the past and didn't forgive them. Well, I knew what to do then! I repented and things were in a flow again. The Bible says forgive.

Mark 11:25 & 26
AND WHEN YE STAND PRAYING, FORGIVE, if ye have ought against any: that your Father also which is in heaven may forgive you your trespasses. But if ye do not forgive, neither will your

Father which is in heaven forgive your trespasses.

DISCERNING YOUR PHYSICAL BODY

God took one day off from His work as an example for you and me. He promised us a long satisfied life, but there are rules we need to follow. You can't keep breaking natural laws and think your body will last. If you don't rest, you'll burn out. It will catch up with you!

> **Genesis 2:2 & 3**
> **And on the seventh day God ended his work which he had made; and he RESTED on the seventh day from all his work which he had made. And God blessed the seventh day, and sanctified it: because that in it he had RESTED FROM ALL HIS WORK which God created and made.**

I used to be a worry-wart, and because I was, I ran around as fast as I could go all the time. That was passed on to me from my mother, but I passed it on to the devil! God said to me that by the age of fifty-nine I'd be dead if I didn't make that change, and all the fruit I was supposed to bring to Heaven would be lost. Think about that! I preach divine healing! Anything I do that's not right affects the body of Christ. I can't go to Heaven yet; I have too many responsibilities. I have to teach these young ministers how to walk in the Spirit and raise up Word and Spirit churches instead of flesh churches. My work isn't finished yet! I tell my body, "I'm not done with you!" When I'm done with my body, I'll lay it down. My body is made to serve me and offer me its supply. But that doesn't mean I can abuse it and treat it anyway I want!

I remember a woman who was married to a well-known Christian motivational speaker. She had been supernaturally healed of cancer, but after a year the cancer returned. I was praying for her with a group of ministers when God told me, "She's going to die." I finished praying with the other ministers, but I knew it wouldn't do any good.

Later, when I was alone in my room, I asked God, "Why is she going to die? Her husband needs her." God told me that she got healed, but went back on the road and wore herself out. When someone recovers from cancer, it takes time to repair their body and gain strength. There's some practical things you have to do. You have to take care of your body and let it rest.

What about being overweight? You get a holy hush on that one when you bring it up in a service. Is God telling you to lose weight? I minister to a lot of people with diabetes, and when I lay hands on them, God says, "They're not going to do anything about it. I've already told them to do something with their body, and they didn't do it." You can't fulfill your part for God if you pack a bunch of extra weight on your body and cause it to break down! That body is the only one you'll have on the earth. If you beat it up, you won't finish your course.

THE SECRET THINGS

> **Deuteronomy 29:29**
> **The SECRET *THINGS BELONG* UNTO THE LORD our God: but those *things which are* revealed *belong* unto us and to our children for ever, that *we* may**

do all the words of this law.

When it comes to you and your family or ministry, God will always let you know why things aren't going right. But when it comes to others, He may not let you know. There are some things that are just none of our business. God has talked with me before about why people die, and told me the causes. There have also been times when He said, "That's none of your business." I tell you what; I'm smart enough to stay out of it when God tells me that!

I had to deal with that when one of my eagle partners got cancer. I was praying for her during her chemotherapy treatments and pleading my case (Isaiah 43:26). I told God, "She's a strong partner, and I need her, so You need her! God, she's only in her forties."

> WHEN IT COMES TO YOU AND YOUR *Family* OR *Ministry*, GOD WILL ALWAYS LET YOU KNOW WHY THINGS AREN'T GOING RIGHT.

The Lord told me, "There are causes for the cancer."

I remember the last time I was at her church before she died. I laid hands on her, and it was like laying hands on a door knob. After the service I went to my room and cried. I said, "She is going to die, isn't she?"

God said, "Yes."

A few weeks later she died, and I finished up a meeting and went to her funeral. After the service, I was in the back room with her husband and some other folks. They started saying they were questioning some things about what happened. I told them, "The secret things belong to the

Lord." I didn't tell them that I knew one of the causes, because they would want to know why, but I knew it was best to hold my peace. You don't have to say everything God shows you or tells you. Sometimes those things are just for you to know!

BEING *Out* OF THE WILL OF GOD

A few years back, I was waking up to get ready for a meeting, but I was so sick I couldn't get out of bed. I was just worn out. God told me to phone ahead and have another minister take my place at the next meeting. He also told me to sleep in, then travel back home, and He'd talk to me about it later.

God gave me two causes why that sickness was able to get in. The first reason was that I didn't rest like He told me to. When I was thirty or forty years old, I could burn the candle at both ends; but I didn't consider my body, and it got me in trouble!

My wife used to watch me as I'd pace around our coffee table with my mind running. She'd say, "You walked around that table fifteen times."

I'd reply, "I did not."

She was right. God told me I would have to put my foot to my flesh and learn how to rest. When He said that, I was responsible to do it.

The other cause was that I wasn't obeying God in the prophet's ministry. I wasn't saying what He told me to say. I wasn't discerning the Lord's body in this area. There were some ministers who were selling phone cards from the pulpit, and God had me speak out against it. I got persecuted big time! Even by some from our faith group. So, I shut up about it. I just wanted to be a sweet teacher and have everyone buy my tapes. I wanted to be one of those ministers who goes into a town, makes everyone laugh, gets people saved, then leaves town. That would be nice, but that didn't go over well with God if I wasn't saying what He told me to say.

> IF YOU HAVE TO TELL EVERYBODY YOU'RE A *Prophet*, YOU'RE PROBABLY NOT.

Sometimes a prophet has to say things that are strong. I didn't ask to be a prophet, but that's what I am. One minister was talking to me one time about how Dad Hagin told him I was going to walk in the office of a prophet. Well, I am now.

A lot of people say they'd like to be a prophet, but they don't want to take the responsibility that comes with that office.

If you have to tell everybody you're a prophet, you're probably not. I had one guy come up in a ministry line and tell me he was a prophet. I asked him if anyone else knew it. If you're truly in a ministry office, more people will know about it than your mother and your spouse.

Well, I paid attention to what God had told me to do for a while, but then I fell back into my old bad habit of not resting. Then a lump appeared in my body. I was at my dentist's office and had him look at it. He didn't think it was anything, but gave me the name of a doctor to have it examined. I forgot all about that note until I found it in my pocket one day. I thought, "I'm not going to do that," but

God interrupted me and told me to go see the doctor. Be sensitive to the leading of the Holy Ghost! It's not doubt and unbelief to have your body looked at. I'm sure glad I did!

I went to the doctor, and he said he couldn't find anything, so I went about my business. But then another lump appeared in my body. The doctor said, "Let me check this out." He had another specialist come in, and they wanted to take a biopsy the next morning. I didn't want them cutting on my body, but God said, "Do it!" Praise God for the Holy Ghost!

When the results came back, they said I had cancer. They wanted to begin treatments and said I may lose my hair. I told them, "I can't do that; I'm a preacher."

I told the doctors that I was going to go home and take care of this. They thought I was in denial, but I didn't deny it was there. I denied its right to stay there!

I went home, sat down in my Lazy Boy recliner, and held my wife's hand. I told her, "We're going to get some answers." I went to the scriptures in First Corinthians 11:28-32.

"BUT LET A MAN EXAMINE HIMSELF, and so let him eat of *that* bread, and drink of *that* cup. For he that eateth and drinketh unworthily, eateth and drinketh damnation to himself, not discerning the Lord's body. For this cause many *are* weak and sickly among you, and many sleep. For if we would judge ourselves, we should not be

**judged. But when we are judged, we are
chastened of the Lord, that we should not
be condemned with the world."**

I questioned God about the cause. I asked, "God, how
did this get in my body? What am I not discerning right?"
The Word says God will satisfy us with long life (Psalm
91:16). I asked the Father, along with my advocate, Jesus,
for answers. I pled my case.

God told me the two causes – not resting my body and
not obeying Him in the prophet's ministry – and I repented.
Then He spoke to me again, "In thirty days it will all be
gone." Glory be to God, it was!

Every year I have a check-up, and they say they can
find no trace of me ever having had cancer. They say I've
been cured of it. They told me, "Somebody up there is
looking out for you." He sure is!

You see, what I was doing in the natural was going to
affect things in the Spirit. If I was a baby Christian, I could
have gotten away with that, but the more you know, the
more responsible you are. Make sure you properly *discern*
the Lord's body, and you can know the *causes* for any wrong
things in your life.

CHAPTER Three

"THINGS THAT PERTAIN TO THE LORD'S BODY"

1 Corinthians 11:29-32, 12:1
For he that eateth and drinketh unworthily, eateth and drinketh damnation to himself, not discerning the Lord's body. For this cause many *are* weak and sickly among you, and many sleep. For if we would judge ourselves, we should not be judged. But when we are judged, we are chastened of the Lord, that we should not be condemned with the world. Now concerning spiritual *gifts*, brethren, I would not have you ignorant.

In the last chapter we learned people are weak, sick, and die early because they don't discern the Lord's body. Not discerning the Lord's body is a *cause*! It's the main reason for the mess most believers are in today. If you want to stay out of trouble, you have to understand the things that pertain to the Lord's body and be right about them. You have responsibilities as a member of the body of Christ. It's not all about you and your family. What about others? What about your brothers and sisters in Christ? Do you help them when they're in trouble or do you just expect them to be there for you? God doesn't want these things to be a mystery to us, but we have to be taught.

We had a baby in our church that went to Heaven. But faith kept that baby alive for seven months, even though the doctors said he wouldn't live past one day. I don't know why he died and don't need to know why. The secret things belong to the Lord!

Our church had a home-going service for the baby, but only a small percentage of our folks came out to it. I told our congregation that it was a shame more of them didn't come out. People don't realize that when the church family gets together, we should all be involved in it. The church is a spiritual thing. It's where things happen and people get changed. If someone is in trouble in the church, we should all jump in and offer a supply.

> **1 Corinthians 12:26**
> **And whether one member suffer, all the members suffer with it; or one member be honoured, all the members rejoice with it.**

Everything we do in the church pertains to the Spirit. Christians can get distracted with fleshly stuff that takes them out of church and away from the Lord's body, and they reap corruption (Galatians 6:7-8). The body of Christ pertains to the Spirit.

FAMILY *Chores*

Just like you have chores in a natural family, you have chores in a church family. Don't be ignorant of your chores. Not finding your part in the Lord's body will lead to trouble.

It's not too much to ask sheep to bring their supply to their local church. Everyone is to do their part.

> **Ephesians 4:16**
> **From whom the whole body fitly joined together and compacted by that which EVERY JOINT SUPPLIETH, according to the effectual working in the measure of every part, maketh increase of the body unto the edifying of itself in love.**

I don't know about you, but I was raised in a family where everyone had chores. You have a job to do! We're saved by grace, but what about works? We're not saved by works, but once we are born again, we're to produce works of faith so we can bear much fruit. Those of us who are word of faith think about homes, cars, health and wealth, which is all right, but what about works?

> **James 2:17 & 18**
> **Even so faith, if it hath not works, is dead, being alone. Yea, a man may say, Thou hast faith, and I have works: show me thy faith without thy works, and I will show thee my faith by my works.**

What about your part in the body of Christ when you retire from your job? Is your commitment to the church supposed to be less then? No! We've got some people in the body of Christ who think when it's time to retire, they should drive around in some RV and look at trees all the time. Now, there's nothing wrong with taking a vacation, but you can look at trees in the millennium. They'll look a lot better then! Why not use all that extra time to volunteer at the church instead of driving around? You don't need to spend all your time running around with your friends looking at a tree. Sometimes it's those friends who hurt your supply to the Lord's body.

I don't believe in friendship, because it's cliquish. I believe in fellowship, because then you can enjoy everyone. When people get caught up in friendships, it causes problems. When the leader of that clique gets disgruntled, he gets the group disgruntled, and they take on his offense. You're supposed to follow your shepherd, not some disgruntled goat! You're supposed to walk away when someone talks about your pastor! You don't want to do anything that hurts the Lord's body!

MINISTERS HAVE TO *Discern* THE BODY OF CHRIST

As someone in fivefold ministry, this applies to me too! I'm just as responsible as a sheep in the local church. Actually, I'm more responsible! As a minister, I have to pay attention to what I do and what I say. My choices have a big impact on what happens to those around me. Over the years, I've seen ministers make decisions that helped the body of Christ, and I have seen others hurt the church. I want to help, not hurt!

What about ministers who have wrong motives and take all sorts of offerings? They say things like, "I have an anointed coat, and when you put money in my pocket, you'll have debt reduction." That's a *cause* for those guys having trouble in their ministries.

I was in a meeting with a guy who wrote one of those prosperity books. During the meeting, he was talking to the people in the congregation about all his physical problems. I told him he should be ashamed to say all that in front of the people. The reason he has physical problems is because he's teaching prosperity things wrong just to benefit himself. He doesn't think how does this affect the local church?

Don't get me wrong. I believe in giving. I believe in debt reduction. I believe in giving to ministers and blessing them. But I don't believe in teaching something wrong just for personal gain, because then you're hurting the body.

How about these ministers who are out running around and drinking alcohol? Today there's an epidemic of those drinking in the church. They have to drink because they are empty.

Ephesians 5:18
And be not drunk with wine, wherein is excess; but BE FILLED WITH THE SPIRIT...

There are some in California who call themselves "the inner circle". They go to Las Vegas to drink and see girly shows. They call it "hangin". I hang with the Holy Ghost! I did all that womanizing and drinking and partying before I got saved, and it wears out fast! Now I serve Joel's stuff, the Holy Ghost (Joel 2:28).

The Holy Ghost and a revival of God never wear out. For forty-three years I've been on a high that the world could never give. Glory be to God! The life of the believer is the most exciting life you could live. If you don't think so, you're thinking wrong! What an honor to be in the ministry and work for God: getting people saved, healed, and filled with the Holy Ghost. It's not a drag; it's an honor!

YOUR *Spouse* AND THE BODY OF CHRIST

People call me and my wife a "dream team" because she helps me. I preach in our church; but I'm not a pastor, she is. Some men call me pastor because they have a problem with a woman being in charge. They're male chauvinists. That's an area where they don't discern the Lord's body. I do! I discern my wife and her part in the church. She's more than just my wife; she's a needed part of the body of Christ.

Sometimes men are just flat mean to their wives. They come to church and prophesy, then go out and treat their wife wrong. They tell her, "I am the head of this house!" You don't own your wife! She's not just a sex object. Listen to her ideas. If you don't, it's like you're saying to Jesus, "Could you move over? I'm another Jesus who knows everything."

> I DISCERN MY WIFE AND HER PART IN THE CHURCH. SHE'S MORE THAN JUST MY *Wife*, SHE'S A NEEDED PART OF THE BODY OF CHRIST.

You may say, "I was raised thinking that women are supposed to be barefoot and pregnant." Well, you're wrong! Don't be one of those guys who gets mad when his food isn't ready right when he gets home from work. Don't be one of those guys who expects his wife to take care of the kids all by herself. You sure enjoyed making those kids, but now you expect her to do all the work? That's not right.

I was raised in a home like that. My dad yelled for his

dinner. He'd sit with a big bowl of popcorn, drinking beer and watching Jackie Gleason on television. He'd say along with Jackie Gleason, "To the moon, Alice!" It seemed like my dad did that weekly to my mom. He was actually training me by that.

When I got married, I did the same thing. I'd say, "Shut up! You can't have an opinion, woman! How can you have an opinion?" I followed the example I saw.

> ...IF YOU'RE WEAK IN A CERTAIN AREA BUT YOUR *Spouse* IS STRONG, SUBMIT TO YOUR SPOUSE IN THAT AREA.

That's why it's important to get around the right kind of men. Get around a man who's a gentleman and let him teach you if you don't know how to do it. You're not called to be a bully. She's your precious wife. When you put down your wife, you're touching the body of Christ. She's made in the image of God (Genesis 1:26). Understand that you can disagree with your wife without being disagreeable. Be a gentleman.

If you're fearful about money and your wife isn't, let her handle the finances. Why do you think you're the only one who has an opinion on how to spend the money? His money should be hers, and her money should be his. Don't be stupid and mishandle the money. Make decisions together.

When Paul wrote in Ephesians 5:21, "Submitting yourselves one to another...", he meant that if you're weak in a certain area but your spouse in strong, submit to your spouse in that area. If she wants to tithe and you don't, let her! Your heart is beating because of God. You can at least give Him ten percent. God has told me about men who died early because they didn't let their wives obey the Word in tithing. Those men didn't discern their part.

We have to discern the *causes* in our marriages. There should never be a divorce in the body of Christ because we have the love of God (Romans 5:5). You can't say, "I can't take it anymore; I'm out of here!" That should never be an issue. You have to both be doers of the Word and honor one another.

There are lots of women who are going to have to face God for leaving their husband when he was serving in ministry. What they did affected the body of Christ. You can't say, "I'm tired of you, and I'm leaving." Now if your husband is beating you, leave him! But if you're just being an old battle axe, you have to consider how your decision will affect the body of Christ.

The same goes for men! The Bible says your prayers will be hindered if you don't honor your wife (1 Peter 3:7). There'll be no new truck if you dishonor her! Your wife belongs to the body of Christ. She's your wife, not your slave. You're in this together.

I remember one time when I was pretty hard on my wife. Later that day, I was in bed praying, and God said, "You're prayers aren't going to be answered until you make that right." Well, I repented and made things right!

Make sure you're quick to repent and quick to forgive! We might as well get all the junk out now, so we can have a long life!

CHAPTER Four

"THINGS THAT PERTAIN TO THE GIFTS OF THE SPIRIT"

1 Corinthians 12:1
Now concerning spiritual *gifts*, brethren,
I would not have you ignorant.

Like I said earlier, when you start reading through First Corinthians 12, you see that the whole chapter is talking about things that pertain to the Spirit and discerning the Lord's body. So, what I want to do is talk about those things as they're brought up in that chapter.

In Chapter 1 we talked about how God, Jesus, and the Holy Ghost work together to bring God's plan to pass. We showed that God is the operator, Jesus is the administrator, and the Holy Ghost is the manifestor (1 Corinthians 12:5-7). Then, in verse eight, Paul starts talking about the gifts of the Spirit. The gifts of the Spirit pertain to the Spirit of God. We have to discern these things if we want to know how they operate and be used in them.

Dad Hagin told us about how there was a minister who said he'd been praying for the gifts to manifest. But Dad Hagin taught us that the gifts don't come by prayer, they come by hunger. Jesus told me these endowments will increase, and there is a time when they'll all work at full potential power, but we have to be hungry for them to manifest.

Your supply doesn't come out of Heaven. God has to speak to a person in the earth to do their part and be a supply to you. That's why it's so important to know how to hear God's voice. When we don't know how to hear His voice, we hinder the flow of supply and the gifts of the Spirit from manifesting.

That has happened to me. God told me that He spoke to one hundred businessmen about buying me an airplane, but they wouldn't obey. One of them got out of the will of God and got himself into some trouble. Today he's in prison because he opened the door to the devil through his disobedience. Because these businessmen wouldn't obey God, I had to start my own business.

God wants to operate on this earth, and Jesus is administrating it; but if you won't obey, the Holy Ghost can't make it happen.

> **Matthew 18:18**
> **Verily I say unto you, Whatsoever ye shall bind on earth shall be bound in heaven: and whatsoever ye shall loose on earth shall be loosed in heaven.**

Something must be done here on earth before Heaven will move. We have our side, and God has His side. The gifts of the Spirit can operate in your daily life if you're yielded to them. God can use the gifts of the Spirit to get you in position to receive your supply spiritually, mentally, and financially.

I know of a businessman who was sitting in a meeting when God gave him a word of knowledge on how to put in his bid for a job. That word of knowledge profited that man because he was walking in the Spirit.

Are you sensitive to the voice of God? Does God want to manifest, but you aren't listening? Have you missed it because you're too distracted? The gifts of the Spirit aren't just for a church meeting; they're for your profit everyday! But they can't help if you won't let them!

THE GIFTS OF THE SPIRIT *Defined*

I'm not against education, but you have to be sure that you don't educate your mind at the expense of your spirit. I'd rather someone be dumb and go to Heaven than be smart and go to hell. We need a good spiritual education.

Some Christians just need a dip! When I was young, I worked on a chicken farm. We used to soak the chickens in a hot tub of water, so we could take off all their feathers. That's what some people need for their heads, a dip to clean out all that religious thinking. They need to shut off their head by praying in the Holy Ghost.

I heard one man who had been saved for thirty years say he'd never heard the voice of God. He may not have heard God, but that doesn't mean God wasn't speaking. That kind of person isn't used in the gifts of the Spirit. God may want to use him, but he's too dull of hearing. That's why we need to be educated spiritually. We need to understand what spiritual things are and how they operate, and that includes the gifts of the Spirit. To better educate ourselves, let's take a look at these gifts one by one.

1 Corinthians 12:8-10
For to one is given by the Spirit the word of wisdom; to another the word of knowledge by the same Spirit; To another faith by the same Spirit; to another the gifts of healing by the same Spirit; To another the working of miracles; to another prophecy; to another discerning of spirits; to another *divers* kinds of tongues; to another the interpretation of tongues:

THE WORD OF WISDOM

The word of wisdom is a portion of God's wisdom concerning the future. It's just a word, not everything. It's not college wisdom, natural wisdom or education. It comes from the Spirit of God to help you know about something coming in the future.

God gave me a word of wisdom years ago as a businessman that saved me some important accounts. I had twelve Burger Kings that my business cleaned. One night God told me that the man who cleans those restaurants wasn't going to show up for work. That man actually got drunk the night before and woke up late. I went down there and got them cleaned. He finally showed up late, after I had done all the work. I would've lost that account if it hadn't gotten done. That gift of the Spirit benefited me!

THE WORD OF KNOWLEDGE

The word of knowledge is a portion of God's knowledge about a past or present situation. It's not intellectual knowledge; it's spiritual.

A word of knowledge can help a parent know where their children are and what they're doing.

This gift has helped us in pastoring our church to know about the motives of people who visit our church. One time we had a guy show up, and God told me he was there to get our girls. I met him at the front door and told him, "You're not going to do that here!" And he didn't! The gifts of the Spirit will help you keep your church and ministry clean if you pay attention.

THE GIFT OF FAITH

The gift of faith is not the measure of faith you get when you're born again (Romans 12:3). When you're born again, you get the measure of faith; and you have to build that measure, so it will grow (Romans 10:17). The gift of faith is different than the measure of faith that every believer has. The *Amplified Bible* calls it "wonder-working faith". When that gift of faith comes, it's like another faith is poured into you, and you can't doubt.

> WHEN THE GIFT OF FAITH COMES, IT'S LIKE AN-OTHER FAITH IS POURED INTO YOU, AND YOU CAN'T *Doubt*.

Sometimes you see God using an evangelist in this area.

Smith Wigglesworth moved in this gift of the Spirit. Those who were around him said you could see it when that gift came on him. He once raised a guy from the dead during the man's own memorial service using this gift. The man was in a casket during the service, and Smith Wigglesworth went directly to the body, pulled the guy out of the casket, and slammed him against the wall. When he did that, he commanded the man to come to life. He did that three times, and on the third time the man came to life.

Another time, a congregation was having a memorial service for one of its deacons who had died. Smith Wigglesworth heard about it and went down to the funeral parlor where they had the body of that deacon. He picked up the man's body, threw it over his shoulder, and carried the man three blocks to the church where the memorial service was taking place. He walked up the center aisle and put the man in a seat on the platform. People were screaming and falling out all over the place! Smith Wigglesworth went to the pulpit and said, "Deacon Jones has a testimony to give." At that moment the dead man opened his eyes and walked up to the pulpit. That's not natural faith; that's the gift of faith!

THERE'S A GIFT OF HEALING FOR *Every* DISEASE UNDER THE CURSE OF THE LAW.

THE GIFTS OF HEALING

The gifts of healings are not one gift, but many. "Gifts" is plural, and each of those individual gifts has a job description. There's a gift of healing for every disease under the curse of the law (Deuteronomy 28). There's a gift of healing for cancer, a gift of healing for asthma; there's a gift of healing for every sickness and disease! This gift of the Spirit is one of the ways to receive your healing.

Many times these gifts of healings don't operate as strong in Word of Faith churches because the people know more and are responsible for what they know. They must use their own faith. That's why I noticed I have more of these gifts operate in denominational churches. They don't know as much about these things.

THE WORKING OF MIRACLES

The working of miracles is when the power of God causes an event that goes against the natural course of nature.

During one of my services, I had a man come up for prayer who didn't have a fully grown thumb. When I ministered to that man, the rest of his thumb grew out. That was a creative miracle.

If someone's missing a body part, they don't need healing. They need a creative miracle because you cannot heal what's not there. It's God working a miracle *through* you.

You will see this gift oftentimes operate in the offices of the prophet and the apostle. You're not an apostle if you don't have miracles.

THE GIFT OF PROPHECY

Prophecy is an utterance that edifies or builds up, exhorts or stirs up, comforts or cheers up (1 Corinthians 14:3). This gift usually comes on the wings of a word of wisdom or a word of knowledge, and they usually come together.

If you see someone giving prophecies all the time, I'd be careful. These things function as the Spirit wills. Discernment in these things is really important because everybody has a mouth, and everybody can talk.

Someone prophesying money out of your pocket or

telling you your address may be doing it by a familiar spirit. Don't you know where you live and how much money you have in your pocket?

Just because you may prophesy, it doesn't make you a prophet!

THE DISCERNING OF SPIRITS

The discerning of spirits is not suspicion. When this gift operates, you're able to see into the spirit world and see both good and evil spirits. Stay away from people who see evil spirits everywhere. They get all devil-conscious and get off. Devils don't bother me. If one gets in my way, I just knock him off!

In Toronto, Canada, I was preaching one time and saw this kangaroo-looking thing with a monkey face. I asked the Lord, "What is that?" He said it was an evil spirit left over from the last administration in that church. He told me to take care of it, and I did. That church has seen nothing but growth since. That church profited withal from that gift of the Spirit.

Another time, I got caught up in the Spirit, and Jesus appeared to me with my mother, who had died years before. He said, "I came to let you know your mother is with Me."

There was also a younger woman standing to Jesus' right. She was the daughter of a minister. She had committed suicide, and the devil was trying to tell the girl's mother that her daughter didn't make it to Heaven. This minister and his wife were in the service that night, and Jesus wanted this mother to know her daughter was with Him. That brought comfort to that family.

I remember the discerning of spirits operating when my mother died. At the time, I had a cleaning business, and I was working that night. While I was working, the smell of that evil spirit that had tormented my mother came in the place. When my mother died, that spirit left her and tried to get on me. I told him, "No way! I know who you are, and you're not getting on me!" And he didn't!

Did you know that evil spirits have smells? One of the dirtiest devils is a homosexual spirit. Even other devils won't hang around with homosexual devils. That's why you have to pay attention to who your kids run with. Just because somebody goes to church, it doesn't mean they're right. Discern these things!

DIVERS TYPES OF TONGUES AND INTERPRETATION OF TONGUES

Divers kinds of tongues and interpretation of tongues equal prophecy. This is not a *translation* of what was said in tongues, but an *interpretation* of what was said.

When my wife and I operate in this gift, I speak in tongues and my wife interprets. In our local church we don't operate in it as much because we know about issues in the church. But the Spirit of God uses us in this mostly as we travel, and it brings blessing and profit to the body of Christ.

THE GIFTS OF THE SPIRIT *Profiting* WITHAL

"I'M BURNING UP! I'M BURNING UP!"

I was in a meeting several years ago in Galveston, Texas, on a Sunday morning. While I was ministering, God wanted to do an operation in that service. God planned it, Jesus administrated it, and the Holy Ghost manifested it through me. He couldn't do it unless He had someone willing to yield. While I was ministering, a man started screaming, "I'm burning up! I'm burning up!"

The ushers began to move toward the man, but I said, "Wait, wait it's the Holy Ghost!"

The man continued, "My face, my neck, my back, my head, they're all burning up!" Suddenly he stopped and said, "They're gone! They're gone!"

He had been in an accident while driving ninety miles per hour and was thrown through the windshield. Because the top of his skull was gone, the doctors had to put a metal plate and screws in his head. During the service, he checked himself, and all the screws and the metal plate were gone. They turned to bone. God also straightened out his face which had been disfigured from the crash. That's the kind of thing God wants to do, but we have to be yielded.

> DURING THE SERVICE, HE CHECKED HIMSELF AND ALL THE SCREWS AND THE METAL PLATE WERE *Gone*. THEY TURNED TO BONE.

During a different meeting, I was laying hands on a man with plates and screws in his body, and God turned those things into bone. That was a different operation of the Spirit than the man who had the car accident because I didn't touch that man. God healed him while I was preaching. But I laid hands on this other gentleman. Paul mentioned this type of anointing in Acts 19:11. *"And God wrought special miracles by the hands of Paul...*"

I call these "specialty anointings". We have to learn how to be skillful in these operations, so people can benefit from them, and so they'll profit withal. I've seen more creative miracles in my ministry than ever before. That's because I pay attention to how these things operate in my life and ministry.

REPLACED PARTS

I was in Lake Charles, Louisiana, and had a professional golfer come up for healing. Some time back, he had fifteen inches of his intestines taken out for medical reasons. After I laid my hands on him, he said he felt a burning sensation in his body and wanted to get checked out by his doctor again. When he went back to his doctor and had some tests done, the doctor told him the missing intestines were back!

"STILL RUNNING!"

In Orlando, Florida, we had a woman receive ministry who had been in a car wreck. I was getting ready to dismiss the service and had a vision of a scar. I told the congregation about it, and a woman responded who had been in an accident and damaged her hip. When she stood up, I saw she had on a large brace. I never laid hands on her, but the power of God began ministering. As I continued with the service, I suddenly saw something out of the corner of my eye go flying. That woman took off the brace and began running around the church! Glory be to God! The doctors said she would never be able to walk without that brace, but I spoke with the pastor later on, and he confirmed, "She's still running!"

"THAT'S MY WIFE"

While in Springfield, Missouri, the discerning of spirits manifested, and I saw an angel standing off to my right during the service. I asked the angel what he was doing there, and he said he had a new heart for a woman. I asked the congregation who needed a new heart, and a dignified looking man stood up and said, "That's my wife." He told me that she was on the bottom of a waiting list for a new heart, and the doctor said she wouldn't get it in time. I told them that God, in His love and mercy, planned for her to receive a new heart. I told them Jesus administrated it, and the Holy Ghost was going to manifest it.

When I laid hands on her, I saw that angel put the new heart into her chest. I later got a letter from them. Their doctor told that couple, "You have someone looking out for you up there because she has the heart of a twenty-two year old." She profited withal from that. If we don't believe in the gifts, nobody profits withal.

THE MAN FROM CHILLICOTHE

One night I was ministering and felt someone needed healing in the area of cancer. I told the congregation about the endowment I received to kill cancer from Jesus when I went to Heaven in 1999. After I told this, a man stood up and came over to where I was.

He said, "Remember me?" I didn't. He continued, "I was in Chillicothe, Missouri, at your meeting, and I was the man you smelled death on. If you remember, they carried me out of a wheelchair for you to minister to me." Glory to God, he'd been completely healed in that meeting! But this night he brought a man with him from California, Missouri, who had cancer and came to be healed. I saw death all over him.

I often see those things in my ministry as a prophet. There's a gray cloud over someone's head when a person is under a heavy test, and a black cloud with a white mask when death is on a person.

The man said, "I came to be healed." Well, I knew he'd get it then! I later heard he was healed, and the doctor told him, "Somebody is sure looking out for you!"

"SAY JESUS"

We were in Kankakee, Illinois, and a girl who was about twenty-two years old came for ministry. She had been deaf and dumb all her life and wanted to be healed. I stuck my fingers in her ears and felt the fire of God jump from finger to finger. I said to her, "Say Jesus." She said, "Jesus." Hallelujah, she began speaking and could hear.

At a different meeting in Houston, Texas, I ministered to a young deaf and dumb girl. After commanding that spirit to come out, I told her, "Say Jesus." She said, "Jesus." Praise the Lord! We are seeing more and more and more and more of these miracles!

A RECREATED EARDRUM

At our annual Fresh Oil Conference in Murrieta, California, Bob Lemon asked me to pray for him after hearing that deaf people were being healed under my ministry. He was deaf in one ear and wanted healing. After I ministered to him, his doctor said his old ear drum was dead, but a new eardrum developed right beside it. The doctor said he didn't know an ear drum would recreate itself. He didn't know it, but God did!

DISAPPEARING SCARS

I ministered to another gal in the Kankakee, Illinois meetings for hearing problems, but she didn't get her healing instantly.

She went home rejoicing in her healing by faith and went to bed. She got up in the morning and for the first time in years heard the birds singing. She was healed!

But that's not all. She had third degree burns all over her body from a burn accident, and had to put heavy make-up on to cover the scars. While in the bathroom getting ready for the day, she noticed she forgot to take her make-up off from the night before. As she tried to wipe off her make-up, she realized she had new skin on her face. Right now her face is clear, and that creative power is moving down the rest of her body, erasing those scars.

I don't know why those scars on the rest of her body are disappearing little by little, but don't get mental about it. Mental folks want to know why God operated in that way. Mental people don't get it because they try to figure everything out. I read it, I believe it, and I am blessed for it! Don't be mental!

CHAPTER Five

"THINGS THAT PERTAIN TO THE LOCAL CHURCH"

DISCERNING *Your* PART AND THE PART OF *Others* IN THE LOCAL CHURCH

1 Corinthians 12:14-24
For the body is not one member, but many. IF THE FOOT SHALL SAY, BECAUSE I AM NOT THE HAND, I AM NOT OF THE BODY; IS IT THEREFORE NOT OF THE BODY? AND IF THE EAR SHALL SAY, BECAUSE I AM NOT THE EYE, I AM NOT OF THE BODY; IS IT THEREFORE NOT OF THE BODY? If the whole body *were* an eye, where *were* the hearing? If the whole *were* hearing, where *were* the smelling? But now hath God set the members every one of them in the body, as it hath pleased him. And if they were all one member, where *were* the body? But now *are they* many members, yet but one body. **AND THE EYE CANNOT SAY UNTO THE HAND, I HAVE NO NEED OF THEE:**

NOR AGAIN THE HEAD TO THE FEET I HAVE NO NEED OF YOU. NAY, MUCH MORE THOSE MEMBERS OF THE BODY, WHICH SEEM TO BE MORE FEEBLE, ARE NECESSARY: And those *members* **of the body, which we think to be less honourable, upon these we bestow more abundant honour; and our uncomely** *parts* **have more abundant comeliness. For our comely** *parts* **have no need: but God hath tempered the body together, having given more abundant honour to that** *part* **which lacked:**

In the first part of the verses listed above, it shows someone who doesn't think that their part in the body is important or needful. Who are you to say your part in the body isn't important?

The following portion of the above scripture passage shows someone who doesn't think someone else's part in the body is needful or important. Who made you God to judge the part of others in the body? Are you telling me that you know better than Jesus? Are you trying to tell me that Jesus doesn't know what He's doing?

We're not all eyes and ears, but we all have a part. If you're not in the right joint, you'll be in trouble. If you're walking in the will of God, the devil can't touch you. People of God should not be having accidents, getting bumps and bruises, and losing money. Those things happen because they're not rightly connected. We're *all* important!

God can bless your life in a greater way when you

understand your part in the body. When you find your place and are faithful to it, God will move for you. Proverbs 28:20 tells us, *"A faithful man shall abound with blessings..."*

Don't miss out on what God has for you by being ignorant of your place, or by criticizing what others do for God. Find your place in the body of Christ and do your part!

This isn't a message to condemn you. It's a message to help you! Some churches call a message like this a message of "spiritual baggage". They don't want anyone to be confronted or challenged. How will we ever grow up if we're never challenged?

This is a message that gives you information on how to walk in things pertaining to the Spirit of God. Think about it. Why in the world would I put a man in my jet to fly it if he didn't know what he was doing? That would be ignorance; it would be illegal, and I'm glad it is. Well, it's the same thing with the power of God. Why would God give someone His power who's ignorant about it? He won't. That's why we have to be educated about these things.

House RULES

1 Timothy 3:15
But if I tarry long, that thou mayest KNOW HOW THOU OUGHTEST TO BEHAVE THYSELF IN THE HOUSE OF GOD, WHICH IS THE CHURCH OF THE LIVING GOD, the pillar and ground of the truth.

There are house rules and a way to act in the house of God. The modernistic church has made the church a natural thing instead of a spiritual thing.

We had a man who visited us from one of those flesh churches. He said they didn't lift their hands or stand up during praise and worship. They weren't praising and worshipping God in their services; they were just being entertained! They were more interested in being entertained than responding and offering their supply to the service. Now, somebody may say, "Well, that's just not my personality to respond." You respond at football games! You can do it for a pigskin! Why can't you do it for Jesus?

I've been in those kinds of churches. Everybody's sick and having trouble. They are churches where they entertain the flesh and tickle the mind. We're supposed to put those things down! We're supposed to feed the spirit of man, not his emotions and carnality! Being a carnal Christian is nothing more than falling off the lettuce truck every day. When you never grow in these areas, you're being a carnal bucket. People like that get offended at a good church and leave. They get offended because they want entertainment and not the Word of God. I don't want to be in a church like that!

> **WE'RE SUPPOSED TO FEED THE *Spirit* OF MAN, NOT HIS EMOTIONS AND CARNALITY!**

I know of churches that allow homosexuality. One man on television was saying, "Jesus loves everybody." He does, but Jesus doesn't accept sin. I won't have two men in my church holding hands while I preach. If they want help, they can be set free, but they weren't born that way. A perverted devil got on them! They are welcome to come to our church to get free, for as they sit under the Word of God, there should be deliverance. But if you permit that homosexual spirit in the church and don't address it, it will run through the church.

TENDING TO THE *Family*

My wife and I pastor our church supernaturally. We allow the gifts of the Spirit to operate, so we can help the people, but also so we can deal with situations before they become a problem. Pastors need to have the gifts of the Spirit in operation.

You have a flesh church when the pastor is always the last one to find out what's going on. As a pastor, you should know by the Spirit what's going on in your church. If you stand in a ministry office, you have the authority for that office and a right to know what's going on.

We don't have a troubled church. Now, there are people in our church who may be going through tests, but the Spirit of God helps us to hold things in order in our church. The Holy Ghost helps us keep it clean.

We don't have trouble with our board members because we only have ministers on our board and not church members.

I remember one time I had a word of knowledge about some members of our congregation and a word of wisdom on how to deal with it. They were at a local restaurant and I saw one couple saying to the group, "Now, we love the Dufresnes dearly." (When they start with that, you know trouble's coming!) They went on to say that we were wrong in the way we taught tithing. They thought you should only tithe on the net and not the gross.

They were also upset that I said you should tithe on all your increase and not just your paycheck. Listen, if someone buys me a suit, I ask how much it cost. Why? So I can tithe on it because that suit is increase. If I get a car given to me, I do the same thing. You give your best. Don't be like Cain who gave God what he wanted Him to have instead of what God wanted. He didn't give his best!

Those folks were causing division. You see, I have a vineyard that God has given me. If you violate my vineyard and hurt my fruit, you can't be allowed to stay unless you repent and make it right. This man and his wife violated my vineyard. I'm responsible to God for the vineyard He gave me and for the fruit it produces.

I told my wife I would preach the next Sunday. I got up and said to the congregation, "I'm going to help you today." And I read Matthew 9:36.

"But when he saw the multitudes, he was moved with compassion on them, because THEY FAINTED, AND WERE SCATTERED ABROAD, AS SHEEP HAVING NO SHEPHERD."

I asked the congregation, "Are you scattered without a *sheep*?" No, you're scattered without a *shepherd*." Congregations are to follow a shepherd, not other sheep.

Then I read Malachi 3 to the congregation to show what the Word said about tithing. After that, I told the congregation what I saw in the vision and what was said at

THINGS THAT PERTAIN TO THE LOCAL CHURCH

the table in the restaurant.

That's why we don't have a troubled church. When the Holy Ghost is allowed to move, the church will be clean, and you'll have a sweet church.

Eventually, that couple left the church. That man and his wife didn't discern the Lord's body.

> WHEN THE *Holy Spirit* IS AL-LOWED TO MOVE, THE CHURCH WILL BE CLEAN, AND YOU'LL HAVE A SWEET CHURCH.

Pastors need to pay attention to the things that try to get in their churches.

I tell ministers to be careful about having preachers come to their churches if something doesn't seem right. Pastors have to guard their flocks! Are those guest ministers going to bless the sheep or fleece them? Will they get your church mailing list and have their ministry hit up your people for money? This stuff happens! Are they going to add to the church or take away from it?

I could have well-known ministers in because I know many of them, but having them in our church wouldn't flow with us. I don't want a variety of ministers with a variety of doctrines to impart into our congregation because it could confuse them.

One pastor called me years ago and asked what I thought about a minister he was going to have in. He said, "I know that some of his doctrines aren't right, but I told him to just teach on faith."

I said, "Sure, but he's going to bring his books and tapes,

and your people will buy them, then they'll get confused." That pastor didn't listen to me. He had that minister in and ended up with a church split.

A pastor has to be sure his sheep are fed right. I won't recommend a minister who isn't going to leave something good in a church. I won't allow a minister in our pulpit who doesn't have a love for the local church and the pastor. You could get by without the other four ministry gifts, but you can't get by without the pastoral office. The pastor is a feeder and a protector. Without a shepherd, sheep open themselves up to all kinds of junk.

CHAPTER Six

"THINGS THAT PERTAIN TO THE FIVEFOLD MINISTRY"

God HATH SET SOME

1 Corinthians 12:28
AND GOD HATH SET SOME IN THE
CHURCH, first apostles, secondarily
prophets, thirdly teachers, after that
miracles, then gifts of healings, helps,
governments, diversities of tongues.

Notice that First Corinthians 12:28 says, "...*God* hath set..." You're not set in the body by your momma, or a board, or some so-called prophet. The apostle, prophet, evangelist, pastor, and teacher are gift ministries, and they're set in the church by God.

There are phases and rooms within each of the fivefold offices. If you want to understand the fivefold ministry gifts, you have to know they each have a job description and what that job description is.

CAUSING THE BODY TO *Grow Up*

Paul talks about the fivefold ministry in Ephesians 4.

This is where we find their job descriptions.

> **Ephesians 4:8, 11**
> **Wherefore he saith, When he ascended up on high, he led captivity captive, and gave gifts unto men. And he gave some, apostles; and some, prophets; and some, evangelists; and some, pastors and teachers;**

Jesus administrated these gifts to men. This is why He gave us these offices of ministry, "*For the perfecting of the saints, for the work of the ministry, for the edifying of the body of Christ*" (Ephesians 4:12).

He gave these gifts "for the perfecting of the saints". That just means that these fivefold gifts help us to grow up and be mature. We're not too mature yet!

We're to grow up, so we can do "the work of the ministry". We all have to learn how to do our part.

As we do the work of the ministry, then there's the "edifying of the body of Christ". When was the last time you edified someone? Is it just up to the ministry gifts to build up the body or do you have a part? You have a part. But you can't do it without the preaching and teaching from these ministry gifts.

> **Ephesians 4:13-15**
> **Till we all come in the unity of the faith, and of the knowledge of the Son of God, unto a perfect man, unto the measure of the stature of the fulness of Christ: That we *henceforth* be no more children,**

tossed to and fro, and carried about with every wind of doctrine, by the sleight of men, *and* cunning craftiness, whereby they lie in wait to deceive; But speaking the truth in love, may grow up into him in all things, which is the head, *even* Christ:

Paul said we would *grow up* in Him in all things. You grow up when you get revelation of the things pertaining to the Spirit! We're not there yet. We still have some work to do in these areas. That means the fivefold ministry gifts are still offering their supply.

Ephesians 4:16
From whom the whole body fitly joined together and compacted by that which EVERY JOINT SUPPLIETH, according to the effectual working in the measure of every part, maketh increase of the body unto the edifying of itself in love.

What about a church where everyone is jointly fit together? Your supply is at your joint. When you're in the right place, you have a measure of power that will edify the body of Christ. There's a force and a power when you're in your joint, and it causes finances, favor, and longevity. That's the kind of church that can get some things done!

Never forget that your spiritual joint is in your local church. Traveling ministers are supplemental vitamins, but your main course comes from your pastor. In my opinion, there are more pastors than other fivefold ministry gifts because we need more pastors.

If you mess with a pastor, you're messing with Jesus. The same goes for the other ministry offices. If you talk about a true prophet, you're talking about Jesus. Talking about men and women of God is a quick way to get disconnected from your supply.

Stay IN YOUR OFFICE OF MINISTRY

1 Corinthians 12:28
And God hath set some in the church, FIRST apostles, SECONDARILY prophets, THIRDLY teachers, after that miracles, then gifts of healings, helps, governments, diversities of tongues.

We have to discern the *order* that God put these gifts in the church. The apostle is a sent one and is listed first for a reason. When you're called to be an apostle but try to go to another office, it won't work. You'll affect your ministry and longevity in the earth. An apostle can actually function in any of the other ministry offices, but is first and foremost an apostle.

Some traveling ministers want to find a church and pastor just because they get tired of traveling. That's being out of order.

When I left my first church and moved to Tulsa, I began my field ministry. If I would try to go back to that lower office of pastor, I'd get in trouble with God and become miserable. You can move in and out of one of those lower offices as needed, but you can't neglect the higher office and stay in a lower office, or you'll get out of order.

A pastor isn't a field ministry because he doesn't roam.

The other four offices primarily have a traveling ministry, but not the pastor. Don't get in trouble by trying to operate in an office you're not anointed to be in.

So many pastors ruin their churches by attending meetings of traveling ministers and getting an appetite for an office they're not called to.

I know of a pastor who went out and bought an airplane, but he doesn't have any meetings to preach at. I have a plane to help me do what I'm called to do, but that's because I'm in the field ministry. In the same way a pastor needs a church building to fulfill his ministry, I need an airplane to fulfill mine. It's nothing more than equipment. I go to different places, with different faces, and different restaurants. It may seem glamorous, but people who go with me are tired after three days because they don't have the grace to do what I do. That's why it's important to stay where your grace is!

When pastors start getting an appetite for the wrong things, it will hurt their churches. I know of one pastor who almost lost his church by getting an appetite for other things.

> WHEN PASTORS START GETTING AN *Appetite* FOR THE WRONG THINGS, IT HURTS THEIR CHURCHES.

Don't try to run with someone just because you think they're "big". You have a big God! Just stay in your joint and bring your supply! If you get distracted by all that you think is big, you can miss out on what God wants you to do.

It doesn't matter if you have twelve thousand people or fifty people in your congregation. You have to be given the grace from God to deal with what you have. What matters the most is that you be faithful with the grace God has given you.

Guard against getting bored in your ministry! When someone gets bored with their ministry or their place in the local church, they get tempted to wander into a place God didn't call them to. So, keep yourself stirred up for the ministry God has called you to. Don't be disqualified by leaving your place of ministry!

GUARD AGAINST GETTING *Bored* IN YOUR MINIS- TRY!

I know a lot of ministers who don't fit because they're trying to function in a place they're not called to. When you're in the wrong place, there's no supply for you there.

Dad Hagin said Jesus told him that ninety percent of His ministers never get into the first phase of the ministry He had for them. He also said that's why many of those ministers die when they're middle age, because they don't get in the will of God. That's not long life. We need to get out of our heads and get the mind of the Lord concerning our phases and rooms of ministry.

Being in an office you're not called to is like taking a shower with your socks on; it just doesn't feel right. When you think you're called to an office, you have to ask, "Where is the fruit that office produces? Where are the gifts that go with this office?" If you're in the right office, there will be the fruit of it. It's dangerous to get out of your office

Years ago, there was a well-known minister who got off. He was trying to be a teacher, but really, he was an exhorter to get people saved (Romans 12:8). Many thought he was an evangelist, but an evangelist has miracles, and he didn't (Acts 8:6 & Acts 21:8). He wasn't an evangelist. But because he tried to be a teacher, he got off. We have to get these things right.

Sometimes people think they're a prophet, but they're not. Most of them just need to serve in the ministry of helps.

Dad Hagin said William Branham was one of the greatest prophets of his time, but Brother Branham wanted to be a teacher. His teaching was off, and it started causing a lot of division. He didn't discern what his teachings were doing to the body of Christ. He was ordained a prophet, not a teacher. He had wrong doctrine and wrong people around him. He thought he was the last days Elijah.

Because of the damage he was causing to the body of Christ, he had to be turned over to Satan for the destruction of his flesh, so that his soul would be saved (1 Corinthians 5:5). If he would've continued causing division in the body of Christ through his wrong teachings, he could have cut himself off from God. God in His mercy didn't want him to reach that point, so He turned him over to Satan for the destruction of his flesh so that his soul would be saved. It's not God's best, but it sure beats going to hell!

STAYING IN *My* OFFICE OF MINISTRY

Today, I walk as an apostle and a prophet in the third room of my fourth phase of ministry. There's more notoriety and influence where I am in ministry now, but the first phase of my ministry started in the ministry of helps, serving my pastor and my local church. Many fivefold ministers begin in the ministry of helps and are promoted as they prove faithful to their man of God. As I get older, it will be lighter and easier for me because I proved myself as a sheep and as a faithful son to my spiritual father.

> AS I GET OLDER, IT WILL BE LIGHTER AND EASIER FOR ME BECAUSE I *Proved Myself* AS A SHEEP AND AS A FAITHFUL SON TO MY SPIRITUAL FATHER.

As I get older, I'm also more responsible for what I teach as I travel. I have to make sure I'm helping mature the sheep. Are we feeders or babysitters? Are we doing things according to the Word or are we doing them because others are doing them? Are we going in the right direction as a staff and ministry?

One of the trademarks of my ministry is that I point to the local church. Dad Hagin told me that if I pointed people to their local church and always deposit something good in that church, then I would always have a place to preach, and I would prosper. And I have! I've stayed with what God has called me to do.

It's such an honor to serve God and be in the ministry. You'll never hear me say, "I don't want to do this anymore" or "I want to do something else."

God wants to operate the office of the prophet in the earth through my life. God never took back the thought of what He wanted to do in my life. I have a voice in the body of Christ as a prophet, and I have to say some things. That's a responsibility that comes with my office.

I was in Pawnee, Oklahoma, for a four day meeting. I opened my Bible and couldn't preach. God said, "I want you to talk about people selling all these gizzard cleaners in the church so they can make money. It's all coming down." I had to speak as a prophet.

God also told me to declare in that service that all these drinking preachers are coming down. Things like that can't happen because it hurts the body of Christ. It's unacceptable to God. Don't tell me you can have wine at dinner! I can show you from the Bible that it's wrong (Proverbs 20:1). Preachers having girls on the side is wrong. If a minister teaches false doctrine, he'll be in trouble. Mark it down! If I don't say these things, I'm not bringing my supply and honoring my office. I have to speak.

THE NEED FOR A *Pastor*

Every person should have a pastor (Matthew 9:37). God put your pastor in your life. He's not there to run your life. He's there to help you. God gave you a pastor, so you can have someone to watch over your soul.

> **Hebrews 13:17**
> **Obey them that have the rule over you, and submit yourselves: for THEY WATCH FOR YOUR SOULS, as they that must give account, that they may do it with joy, and not with grief: for that *is* unprofitable for you.**

Jesus isn't your pastor because He doesn't live here anymore. He put gifts in men and women for us, and one of those gifts is the gift in your pastor. You need a pastor who's preaching a sermon to you. You can't be pastored by a television preacher. A preacher needs to see your face for you to be pastored. Paul stated in First Thessalonians 3:10,

"...That we might SEE YOUR FACE, and might perfect that which is lacking in your faith."

THE PASTOR HAS A *Family* HE'S WITH ALL THE TIME AND HE HAS TO REMIND THEM OF THE BASICS ALL THE TIME.

Brother Hagin said in these last days that the shepherd will open up the Bible and teach, and the buildings won't be able to hold all the people who will come. That's a spiritual thing. God pulls them in, not entertainment, or a donkey show, or the blessed nursery. It will be by the Spirit of God.

A pastor's job isn't real glamorous. An evangelist can seem more spectacular because of the miracles and things happening in his ministry. The pastor has a family he's with all the time, and he has to remind them of the basics all the time.

Have you ever noticed that when a child goes to someone else's home, they love it? But when they come home and have chores, they're not as excited. That happens to pastors too. A pastor is parenting.

A sheep may attend the meeting of an evangelist who has a nice jet, and be all excited, and decides that their church services should be like the evangelist's services. Then they go back to their church and hear their pastor teaching messages on being right and living right, and they decide that pastor doesn't have any love, so they leave the church. People like that are nothing more than "church tramps". A "church tramp" has no spiritual father or pastor. They jump from church to church to church. So do their own kids! They end up perverted and messed up because they don't discern the importance of the pastor.

I personally believe a pastor is more important than any other fivefold ministry gift. I'm not taking away from any minister who's doing his part, but it's not the evangelist who lives with the sheep and tends to their needs. He's not the one that's going to visit the sheep in the hospital. He's not going to come to your daughter's wedding either. Your pastor is! He's an important supply for your life.

A pastor's office deals with a lot of routine. They go to the same building, minister to the same people, and do the same things over and over and over. And they do it for you and your family!

I remember hearing of an 82 year old pastor who taught the same message for two years. After a while, the board called him in and wanted to talk with him. They thought he was senile. They asked why he had been preaching the same message for two years. He said, "When you get it, I'll go to something else." He put it back on them.

Another pastor I know loved his people, but wasn't a very good Bible teacher, so every few months he'd bring in a teacher and have a teaching seminar. He discerned what his people needed. He really loved those sheep, and they really loved him. But not all ministers have the same love for the local church as this pastor showed.

WHAT'S YOUR *Motive*?

Have you ever noticed how some of these guys who teach on debt reduction all have nice boats and airplanes? They tell people that if they give to their ministry, their debt will be reduced. Those guys are looking for money!

As a pastor I've seen people go to those meetings, give their money, and come back to church asking for help to pay their mortgage and light bill because they gave all their money away to one of these guys. They didn't get out of debt! They got into bigger debt!

> I BELIEVE IN PROSPERITY, BUT YOUR PROSPERITY IS CONNECTED TO YOUR *Local* CHURCH.

I knew it wouldn't work for these people because they were undisciplined with their money. Even if they did get out of debt, they'd go right back into it. I'd ask them, "Well, did you come out of debt?"

They'd say, "No."

Then I'd asked, "Did you give your tithe to them?" And they'd answer, "Yes."

You see, these sheep and those ministers are not discerning the Lord's body. The supply those people were supposed to be giving to their local church was given to the wrong joint. The people ended up in worse financial shape. Their actions didn't profit withal, and those ministers ended up hurting the local church.

I believe in prosperity, but your prosperity is connected to your local church. When the sheep tithe and give offerings in the local church, then there will be enough for the local churches and for the other fivefold ministries.

As I travel around the country, I find that half of the churches aren't shepherded by true pastors. You can tell by the way they talk about the sheep.

Years ago, I was going to have a revival in one church, and when the pastor picked me up from the airport, he said, "If I had a rope long enough, I'd hang this church." He called them stupid, and I thought, "They're stupid for following you!" That's not a shepherd. He's just getting their wool.

The last time I saw Dad Hagin, I asked him about this. I told him it seemed about half of the churches I visited were being pastored by someone who didn't stand in the office of a pastor. He said that he saw that same thing in all his years of ministry. These men should be a second man, an administrator, or helping in the church, but they're not pastors.

We've got to get these things right if we're going to have barns to hold the precious fruit of the earth! God is putting His precious fruit in Word and Spirit churches so that His fruit remains. Why would God put His fruit in a flesh church and lose His fruit? That's why the fruit won't stay in those seeker-friendly churches. They're run by businessmen who run their churches like a business. God wants to put His fruit in a church run by a real pastor.

CHAPTER Seven

"THINGS THAT PERTAIN TO THE MINISTRY OF HELPS"

1 Corinthians 12:28
And GOD HATH SET SOME IN THE CHURCH, first apostles, secondarily prophets, thirdly teachers, after that miracles, then gifts of healings, HELPS, governments, diversities of tongues.

God sets the members, you and me, in the body as it pleases Him. We don't set ourselves in the body, God does! If it pertains to the body, it pertains to the Spirit. Paul is talking about the body in this verse – the *whole* body.

In the above verse, you see "helps" mentioned. The ministry of helps is a ministry office because it is mentioned with the other offices in First Corinthians 12:28. But it's not a fivefold office because it's not mentioned in Ephesians 4:11.

I say the ministry of helps is the hand that holds up the fivefold ministries. We need more in the helps ministry than in the fivefold ministry because they help the ministry do its job. There is an endowment to help, and there is prosperity that comes with walking in that endowment.

Everyone who walks in his ministry of helps office, and gets his mouth in line with that office is blessed. But you have to keep your mouth in line with what God calls you to do and not be a complainer. There are spiritual phases for laymen to fulfill, but their mouths can cut those things short. A faithful person helps, even if he doesn't understand every decision that's made. He keeps his mouth shut against anything negative and is blessed for it!

Everybody in the church has a job and a supply to offer. The devil wants to get people out of their joint through offense and carnal thinking, so they won't bring their supply. When we come together, God can come in and move and work in some things. But if Satan gets you out of joint and keeps you from bringing your supply, then you cut off the supply for yourself and your needs.

> **Colossians 2:19**
> **And not holding the Head, from which all the body by joints and bands having nourishment ministered, and knit together, increaseth with the increase of God.**

God anoints you to be a supply, and supplies what you need for your position. If you're a door greeter, you have a right to be blessed.

Our job is to discern our part in the body. You have to find your place! How do you do that? Start with your natural abilities. What are the areas you're strong in? Everyone is stronger in some areas than others. Come into the church and start helping with your natural abilities. When you do, you'll end up in your supernatural abilities. Some people say, "I don't need anybody." They're lying.

You do need somebody. If you're not connected, you'll dry up!

Disconnected folks don't bring a supply. They always say, "I'm busy." Sure they're busy, but that's a trick of the devil to keep them out of the things of the Spirit and out of the blessing. My wife always says, "Be in church and bring your supply." She's right.

Do you ask, "Do I have to go to church?" If you do, I have to wonder if you're saved. The reason a person has to ask that is because they're empty and have no fellowship with God.

SOME PASTORS DON'T TEACH THEIR PEOPLE TO DO THEIR PART, AND THAT'S WHY THOSE PASTORS GET *Burned Out*.

Some Christians have a problem being part of the church family because they had a bad home life in the natural. They had a daddy or mommy who left, or they lived in a home full of selfishness and divorce. God's family shouldn't be that way. Those people have to be taught about the church family and being a part of it. Some pastors don't teach their people to do their part, and that's why those pastors get burned out. It's the pastor's fault. People in your church need to be a part of what is going on, but they have to be shown how to do that.

We have a good ministry of helps department at our church, and we let them know we appreciate them. I let them know it's a dignified thing they're doing.

I'm going to think soberly about that office of the ministry of helps because it's important. There are practical things to walking in the Spirit, and the ministry of helps assists in that area.

I was talking with one pastor who told me everyone in his church was a prophet. This guy had a church of 1200 people! I don't even know if there are 1200 prophets in the earth today. If you have a whole church of prophets, how does anything ever get done? Who cleans the toilets? Who teaches the kids? Who passes the bucket? No, you can't have a church full of the fivefold ministry. You can have a large number of them, but a church won't run right without the ministry of helps.

Being A SUPPLY

I remember the time when a deacon board had to deal with the sin of their pastor. The pastor blew it, got in the flesh, and committed adultery. He and his wife worked it out and decided to stay together, but he thought he should offer his resignation to the board. He explained that he would submit to another minister until God said he could be restored.

One of the deacons spoke up and said, "Pastor, you've been here for twenty-five years, and you're the one who pioneered this church. I believe you should stay right here." This deacon didn't crucify his man of God. He saw that the pastor had truly repented. There was maturity in his reaction and view. He said, "Now, nobody else knows about this, so we'll just keep it to ourselves and allow you to be restored."

I believe that if an issue takes place in secret, it should be dealt with in secret. If it's done publically, it should be dealt with publically.

If a person doesn't want to repent, that's a different deal;

but that was not the case with this pastor. All the board agreed, and the pastor was restored. That board member was a supply to the local church and a supply to his pastor. He was a true ministry of helps person who prayed and had the heart of a good sheep. That's why pastors have to be careful to have spiritual men around them.

If you're in a minister's family, be sure you're a supply and don't get a spirit of familiarity. That's dangerous. My wife understands and discerns that. She was a supply when I married her, and she still is! She's not a griper and complainer. Too many ministers have to deal with that in their families, and it hurts the supply they're supposed to be bringing to the body of Christ. Isaiah 10:27 tells us that *"the yoke shall be destroyed because of the anointing."* Don't become a yoke to your man of God, or you'll be removed.

> THAT'S WHY PASTORS HAVE TO BE CAREFUL TO HAVE *Spiritual* MEN AROUND THEM.

One time, I was going back to the hotel after a meeting, and God started talking to me about the couple pastoring the church where I was ministering. He told me how they had been such a supply to their man of God. They loved their pastor, they loved the pastor's children, and they loved the church. I've never heard them say a negative thing about their pastor, but their pastor had made poor decisions, and as a result, died premature. Today they are the pastors of that church. They didn't steal the church; it was given to them due to the attitude of their heart. People like that are valuable.

Some time ago, when this man who became the pastor

had a stroke, I went to God to plead my case, "I need that man. He's a supply to my life." I asked God to give him fifteen more years. That man is a supply to my life. Those pastors are a joint of supply to my ministry and my life personally. Through that joint I was able to plead my case for him. I can't do that for everyone because not everyone will keep their mouth shut when their pastor makes a mistake. This family did, and they were blessed for it!

When I was in the ministry of helps, I didn't speak against my pastor either. I got turned on to God, and I wanted to be a supply. I didn't even know what a supply was back then!

I would go down to Teen Challenge and help with drug addicts on Thursday night. Then I'd go to the Full Gospel Businessmen's breakfast on Saturday. I did all that and was still involved in the ministry of helps at my local church!

MY *Supply* WAS GIVEN BECAUSE I WAS IN THE CHURCH DOING WHAT I COULD DO.

I was the foreman on a construction project at the church, but they weren't paying me. I never told the people in the church about it. That would hurt the church, and people could be mad at the church. God took care of me and my family anyway.

God had me to go behind the local grocery store where they were throwing good food out because of the expiration date. Well, a guy caught me getting the food, and the next night he had five palettes stacked with boxes of food. There was so much food that I collected, that I was giving it away. My supply was given because I was in the church doing what I could do.

> **Matthew 6:33**
> **But seek ye FIRST the kingdom of God,**
> **and his righteousness; and all these**
> **things shall be added unto you.**

When you seek God first and His way of being and doing right, all the things you need will make their way to you. If you're not getting your supply, I would see if I was seeking the right thing.

THE MINISTRY OF *Giving*

There's also a ministry of giving, and we need that office to help fund the vision of the pastor.

> **Romans 12:6, 8**
> **Having then gifts differing according to**
> **the grace that is given to us, whether**
> **prophecy, *let us prophesy* according to**
> **the proportion of faith; Or he that**
> **exhorteth, on exhortation: HE THAT**
> **GIVETH, LET HIM DO IT WITH**
> **SIMPLICITY; he that ruleth, with**
> **diligence; he that sheweth mercy, with**
> **cheerfulness.**

The ministry of giving is a spiritual thing. It affects the body of Christ and helps things get done in the earth.

There are some people we can see walking in this office of ministry. The owner of Chick-fil-A, Mr. S. Truett Cathy, has taught his Sunday school class for fifty years. He doesn't have his stores open on Sunday because he honors God.

He asks, "How can I tell my Sunday school kids to come to church on Sunday and have my registers running?"

His stores sell more chicken in six days than Kentucky Fried Chicken sells in seven days! When he had only one restaurant, he proved himself faithful. That's why he's blessed financially and funds his pastor's vision.

The owner of Hobby Lobby, Mr. David Green, gave Oral Roberts seventy million dollars. They said he was shaking under the power of God when he gave that check to Oral Roberts at a board meeting. He said he was honored to be in the presence of such a man of God and was tired of hearing folks talk bad about him. He said, "I'll get all the bills caught up and be a supply." Praise God! Oral Roberts, at ninety years of age, got all his bills paid!

You see, these men were proven when they just had a little bit of money. They want to fund the pastor's vision. Every church needs some of these men, but fear often hinders them. Fear didn't hinder these men. They're billionaires today because they were proven.

> YOU SEE, THESE MEN WERE *Proven* WHEN THEY JUST HAD A LITTLE BIT OF MONEY.

People who work day and night, but are failing to put God first, don't get it. Most of them are working night and day, but they're not getting their supply because they're not bringing their supply to the local church. They've turned to a natural supply.

Warren Hubs got an idea in a dream. He's a man who gave ninety percent of his income to the church and lived very well on ten percent. Another man named Letourneau Turnapull was given a dream from God about how to make those earth scrapers. He lived off ten percent of his money and gave ninety percent to the work of God. He would've been a trillionaire today. These guys were blessed because they put first things first and took care of the house of God!

Living in the Spirit is where real prosperity is. Living rich is having a full supply of what God has for you. I'm a money magnet because I put God first. If you don't put God first, the only thing added to you is sorrow and lack!

> **Proverbs 10:22**
> **The blessing of the LORD, it maketh rich, and he addeth no sorrow with it.**

CHAPTER *Eight*

"THINGS THAT PERTAIN TO YOUR SUPPLY"

I've received many impartations over the years from my spiritual father, Kenneth Hagin, and my pastor, Dr. Sumrall. I received a supply from them because I followed God and did what He called me to do. I made some mistakes, but I just kept on moving. The steps you take are important to getting where God wants you to be. I want to talk about how God got me with these great men, and how I got where I am today.

MOVING *Toward* A SUPPLY

Years ago I worked with a guy in construction named Billy Frazier. He was an old rodeo cowboy and was always talking to me about Jesus. He'd say, "Jesus loves you, Ed, and I love you too." I thought he was a little weird because men weren't supposed to tell each other that. I told him I was Catholic, but he didn't care. He'd say, "Jesus loves Catholics." He kept asking me to come to his church and wouldn't let up. Just to get him off my back, I finally told him I'd go.

I went to Billy's church but couldn't tell you a thing the preacher said. To me he just sounded like an auctioneer with a bunch of people saying "amen" and "hallelujah." In my Catholic church, one of the sisters would whack you for that!

But at one point in the service, a little Filipino woman stood up and started speaking in tongues. I didn't understand what was going on, but the hair on the back of my neck stood up! I knew it was supernatural, and I knew it was God. The preacher and Billy just dropped their heads because they thought that woman would scare me away, but that's the thing I remember most about the service. After she was done, her husband got up and interpreted what she said in tongues. He said, "Now's the time of salvation." I knew that was for me, and when the pastor gave the altar call, I went forward to get saved.

> I KNEW ENOUGH TO KNOW IT WASN'T RIGHT FOR THE *Pastor* TO BE DOING EVERYTHING.

I went back to the service that night and asked the pastor what I could do to help in the church. He was shocked. He said that he didn't have anyone to clean the toilets, so I told him I'd be glad to do it. That night I started out in the toilet ministry, but I wanted to do more because I was just happy to be a part of the church family.

I asked the pastor if I could clean the carpets, but he said he did them. You see, the pastor did everything. He was like a fire truck running all over because the people didn't do their part. I told him he shouldn't be doing all that stuff. All I knew from the Bible was out of my Catholic background, but God taught me about being a part in the body. I knew enough to know it wasn't right for the pastor to be doing everything. Some of those folks who'd been there for years didn't have a clue about that!

I started my first phase of ministry that night when I began working in the church. I just had a love for God, and He led me to my supply in that local church. If I hadn't taken those steps, I wouldn't be in the ministry today.

I used to go somewhere every night drinking beer and chasing girls for the devil. Now that I was born again, I wanted to do something for God!

What's the problem with Christians who are too tired to come to church? When they were unsaved, they were never too tired to run around for the devil.

I'd go to prayer meetings at church every time we had them. I'd go to Teen Challenge on Thursday nights and help minister to the drug addicts even after I'd worked all day. I'm older now, but I still have that love for God.

I've kept my fellowship with God right all these years, and that's why I've stayed with it. I've had opportunities to be bitter. I've had family leave me, but I decided not to be bitter, and I forgave. If I hadn't forgiven, I would have aborted all that God had for me.

Bringing MY SUPPLY

Billy Frazier, who took me to that Full Gospel church, showed me what God's Word said about tithing.

> **Malachi 3:8-11**
> **Will a man rob God? Yet ye have robbed me. But ye say, Wherein have we robbed thee? In tithes and offerings. Ye** *are*

**cursed with a curse: for ye have robbed
me, *even* this whole nation. Bring ye all
the tithes into the storehouse, that there
may be meat in mine house, and prove
me now herewith, saith the LORD of
hosts, if I will not open you the windows
of heaven, and pour you out a blessing,
that *there shall* not *be room* enough *to
receive it*. And I will rebuke the devourer
for your sakes, and he shall not destroy
the fruits of your ground; neither shall
your vine cast her fruit before the time
in the field, saith the LORD of hosts.**

I thought, "Okay, no problem." Some people had an issue with that. I didn't!

I'd go to church as a Catholic on Christmas and Easter and give $1 in the offering, and then I'd lie on my income tax. It was time to do it right, so I started tithing as soon as I got saved.

All these acts of obedience moved me further and further into the will of God. If I'd withheld my supply, there wouldn't have been a supply for me when I needed it.

Sometime later, God told me to be the foreman on the construction of our new church building. When I told the pastor, he said that God told him the same thing, but there wasn't any money to pay me. I thought, "He doesn't expect me to do it for nothing, does he? I have a family to feed." But I heard from God, and it didn't matter if my whole family thought I was crazy. I was obeying God!

The first month was fine, but after that, we began to get

behind on our mortgage. During the third month I called the church secretary and told her to let the pastor know I was quitting and getting a job to feed my family. I loaded up my tools in the car, went down to the local workers union and got a job assignment, but then I started crying. There I was, crying in a hall full of men. I asked God, "What's wrong with me?"

He said, "I told you to build that church."

I answered back, "You said You'd take care of me and my family." He didn't answer.

When you give your life to Jesus, you don't belong to yourself anymore. If He says it, do it! God will never let you down when He gives you an assignment. God was teaching me how to believe Him for finances and a supply.

I told the main guy at the hall that I couldn't take the job, and he called me stupid. He said, "You have to feed your family!" I knew that.

As time went on, God told me to go behind the Safeway supermarket to find food for my family. I thought, "Doesn't He know I have to pay rent?"

> IF HE SAYS IT, DO IT! GOD WILL *Never* LET YOU DOWN WHEN HE GIVES YOU AN ASSIGNMENT.

When I went behind Safeway, I found stacks of dented cans of food, day old bread, and all sorts of other food to be thrown away. I took the food. The next night, I came back again, and found more food. While loading up, a man came out and said, "So, you're the one taking the food." I explained what I was doing, and the next night he had a forklift of food waiting for me. It took me five trips to get it all home. I had so much food, I was giving it away. Every night that man had food waiting for me! Glory to God!

Everything that pertains to life is already on this earth, and it belongs to you. You'll get the desires of your heart when you're in the will of God and in your joint of supply.

Later on, a man asked me to help him with his cleaning business. He didn't know I needed money for my mortgage, but God was making a way for me. I took the job, and after working on the church all day, I'd clean medical offices.

I cleaned for that guy for a while, then he stopped coming to church. He also stopped paying my salary, so I stopped cleaning! Not long after that, one of the businesses I had cleaned called my church and wanted to know if I would take over the cleaning contact that my boss had since he had ended up leaving town. The next day, another business called and asked me to clean for them. In two months time, I had my own cleaning business and was making $10,000 a month in 1969. Through it all, I always tithed, even on the food from Safeway. I got caught up on all my bills, had three business trucks and fifteen employees, while still working as the foreman on our new church building. Faith does whatever it takes!

Receiving MY SUPPLY

When we were completing the church building, a man gave me a brochure to a Full Gospel Businessmen's Meeting in Colorado. God told me I needed to be in that meeting, so

I sold my house to get the money for the trip, and then moved into a rental home. I didn't know it, but I was getting ready to go into my second phase of ministry.

At the meeting, I heard three men who would have a profound impact on my life and ministry: Kenneth E. Hagin, John Osteen, and Kenneth Copeland. I didn't have the teaching then I do today about being led by the Spirit, but I had a heart for God, and He guided me to the right supply.

I started out by *building* a church, but now I'm *speaking* in church buildings all over the world!

While at that meeting, God spoke to me about those three men. He said Brother Copeland would be one of my teachers, and I should follow his teachings on the blood covenant. He told me I should pay close attention to Pastor Osteen because I would pastor one day, and I should do it the way he did – supernaturally! (I rebuked the thought about pastoring because I saw the way people treated my pastor, and I didn't want anything to do with it! But God was right.) Then He brought me to the third man, Brother Hagin. God said that I should follow him the closest and that he was to be my spiritual father. Over the years, Brother Hagin taught me, and that's how I learned to have longevity in ministry. God put me with a man who was balanced and not flaky.

As a minister you have to guard against letting your attention to your spiritual father dwindle.

1 Corinthians 4:15 & 16
For though ye have ten thousand instructors in Christ, YET HAVE YE NOT MANY FATHERS: for in Christ

Jesus I have begotten you through the gospel. Wherefore I beseech you, be ye followers of me.

I didn't leave my man of God. From 1971-2003, I followed Dad Hagin. I also stayed with Dr. Sumrall until he went home to be with the Lord. I got impartations from these men to take to this generation (Romans 1:11).

When I went to Heaven in 1999, God told me I'd be a leader in this last day revival. He said, "Ministers will flock to you, and you bless them! Put something in them!" You know, you had to have something put in you to be able to put it in someone else.

That's why we have Fresh Oil Fellowship, a ministerial fellowship. When you become a daddy, you have responsibilities. You can't be a dead-beat dad. I have to discern my part as a dad, just like others have to discern their part as a spiritual son or daughter.

I never robbed my spiritual dad. The tithes of my church went to him. My personal tithes went to the church, but the church tithe went to him, and we were so blessed by it.

Protecting YOUR SUPPLY

Sometimes sons can get bored with their fathers. They say things like, "I hear that all the time," when their father is talking. They're missing it!

There are things I had heard Dad Hagin say for years. Then, all of a sudden, I would hear him say it, and I got something new. I loved it when Dad Hagin would get up and tell his stories. The stories are where you get the nuggets.

He would begin a story, and I would turn to my wife and say, "Here we go." Revelation comes when you hear. Don't get bored with hearing.

Lots of young preachers start with me, get a measure of blessing, think they can do what I do, and then they leave. They think they can do it better. They're not hungry, and they're not humble. They're like Lot who left Abraham (Genesis 13:1-11). When Lot's guys and Abraham's guys started fighting, Abraham wanted to avoid strife, so he gave Lot what he wanted. Lot had to go because strife would have shut down the blessings of God. Lot should have sold his cows and fired the guys causing the strife, but he didn't.

> **James 3:16**
> **For where envying and strife *is*, there *is* confusion and every evil work.**

Lot made a big mistake. He forgot that the blessing on his life was connected with his man of God.

Today, some of those young preachers who left too soon are headed down that same path. I've had men violate my vineyard and end up like Lot. They don't want to live right like me, but they sure want what God's blessed me with.

People leave their supply because they're ignorant of their part in the body and the importance of being in the right place in the body. It'll cost them the same way it cost Lot. When people don't properly discern the Lord's body, they become weak, sick, and die early. If you're weak, why? If you're sick, why? These are warning signs that something's wrong.

That happened to me one time. I pulled back from going

to Dad Hagin's meetings because of some other folks, not because of him. I let offense and hurt separate me from my supply. I stayed away for nine months and started to dry up. My wife said, "You'd better get back in his meetings."

God told me the same thing. He said, "You won't go any further in your phases of ministry until you get close to him again." I made that change and got things right. After that, I made it a point to protect my supply and not let anything separate me from what God had for me through my man of God.

You'd better make that same decision! If you don't, the devil can run you off and you'll become easy prey for him!

> **Ezekiel 34:5**
> **And they were scattered, because *there is* no shepherd: and they became meat to all the beasts of the field, when they were scattered.**

CONCLUSION

1 Corinthians 12:1
Now concerning spiritual *gifts*, brethren,
I would not have you ignorant.

Amplified Bible
Now about the spiritual gifts (the special
endowments of supernatural energy),
brethren, I do not want you to be
misinformed.

If we don't want to be ignorant of the things that pertain to the Spirit, we need to be good students. I want to be a good student and not just sit there like a bale of hay! People in Word and Spirit churches should be good students and become "hundred fold" dirt. According to the parable of the four different kinds of dirt (Mark 4:14-20), seventy-five percent of those born again have dirt that doesn't produce fruit. They don't produce fruit because they don't do the Word. I sat in meetings with preachers and heard the same things they did, but I saw them fail. Why? They were bad students. They didn't learn a thing, and it cost them!

We have to discern the Lord's body. What's my part? What's your part? It's because we don't discern these things that *causes* take place. If we judge ourselves, we won't be judged.

> **1 Corinthians 11:29-31**
> **For he that eateth and drinketh unworthily, eateth and drinketh damnation to himself, not discerning the Lord's body. For this cause many *are* weak and sickly among you, and many sleep. For if we would judge ourselves, we should not be judged.**

What's your part in the body? What gifts of the Spirit does God want to manifest through you? What are you supposed to be putting your hand to in the local church? Are you a supply or a siphon? These are things we need to know because they pertain to the Spirit. If we don't know them, the devil can bring weakness, sickness, and early death.

I don't want any of those things in my life. I'm going to finish my course! I'll keep my body under. I'll renew my mind. I'll obey in the offices of ministry. I'm not going to be ignorant concerning the things that pertain to the Spirit!

> **Colossians 1:9-10, AMP.**
> **For this reason we also, from the day we heard of it, have not ceased to pray *and* make [special] request for you, [asking] that you may be filled with the full (deep and clear) knowledge of His will in all spiritual wisdom [in comprehensive insight into the ways and purposes of God] and in understanding and DISCERNMENT OF SPIRITUAL**

THINGS - That you may walk (live and conduct yourselves) in a manner worthy of the Lord, fully pleasing to Him *and* desiring to please Him in all things, bearing fruit in every good work and steadily growing *and* increasing in *and* by the knowledge of God [with fuller, deeper, and clearer insight, acquaintance, and recognition].

My first pastor was my supply when I first got saved, but God had to put me with others who could bring me into more. I faithfully served my pastor, but God had places for me to go, and that pastor couldn't take me there. That's why God hooked me up with Dad Hagin and Dr. Sumrall. I would've never gotten into some spiritual places if it weren't for their supply.

There were still things Dad Hagin tried to get the body of Christ into and couldn't. That's why some of us are preaching this message so hard. If we don't get into these phases and rooms of the Spirit, we'll miss out on what God wants to do.

I'm not going to miss out! I stayed with my supply and got what I needed to finish my course.

Are you with the right supply? Are you receiving from the supply in your pastor? Are you protecting the supply they bring to your life? If you aren't, you won't finish your course. Why? You're not discerning the Lord's body and who God put into your life to help you. If that happens, what will be the results? The results will be weakness, sickness, and premature death. Don't let that be you.

Discern your place in the body of Christ. Bring your supply to the body of Christ. God has more for us, and we can only move into those things as we become skillful in the things that pertain to the Spirit.

ABOUT THE AUTHOR

Dr. Ed Dufresne is a bold, and compassionate minister, with over 45 years experience in the ministry. In 1971, God put a tangible healing anointing in his right hand, and since that time he has traveled over 11 million air miles carrying that healing anointing to this generation.

In 1999, Dr. Ed Dufresne had a vision of heaven, and at that time God gave him an endowment to kill cancer. Since then, there has been an increased number of dramatic healings from cancer recorded.

It has been said of Dr. Dufresne that he has a unique ability to draw the anointing and gifts out of ministers. His annual Fresh Oil Conferences draw ministers from around the globe who come and receive impartations from a man of God whose ministry is earmarked by the moving of the Holy Spirit.

Dr. Dufresne's heavenly assignment has been enlarged in this decade to go to the nations. With a heart for the harvest, Dr. Dufresne travels extensively encouraging the Body of Christ to get ready for the last days move of the Holy Spirit, which will usher in the harvest and mark the return of the Lord!

BOOKS BY DR. DUFRESNE

Devil Don't Touch My Stuff
Faithfulness: The Road to Divine Promotion
Golden Nuggets for Longevity
Praying God's Word
The Footsteps of a Prophet
There's a Healer in the House

For a complete list of CDs, DVDs, and books by Dr. Ed Dufresne, or to be on his mailing list, please write:

Ed Dufresne Ministries
P.O. Box 1010
Murrieta, CA 92564

(951) 696-9258
www.eddufresne.org

BOOKS BY
NANCY DUFRESNE

A Supernatural Prayer Life
Daily Healing Bread from God's Table
God: The Revealer of Secrets
His Presence Shall be My Dwelling Place
Responding to the Holy Spirit
The Healer Divine
There Came a Sound from Heaven:
        The Life Story of Ed Dufresne
Victory in the Name
Visitations from God

For a complete list of CDs, DVDs, and books by Nancy
Dufresne, please write:

Ed Dufresne Ministries
P.O. Box 1010
Murrieta, CA 92564

(951) 696-9258
www.eddufresne.org